Natural Basketry

Natural Basketry

by Carol and Dan Hart

WATSON–GUPTILL PUBLICATIONS, NEW YORK

Copyright © 1976 by Watson-Guptill Publications

First published 1976 in the United States and Canada by Watson-Guptill Publications
a division of Billboard Publications, Inc.
1515 Broadway, New York, N.Y. 10036

Library of Congress Cataloging in Publication Data
Hart, Carol, 1944–
    Natural basketry.
    Bibliography: p.
    Includes index.
    1.   Basket making.   I.   Hart, Dan, 1941–   joint
author.   II.   Title.
TT879.B3H37   1976   746.4′   75–35689
ISBN 0-8230-3154-3
ISBN 0-8230-3155-1 pbk.

Manufactured in U.S.A.

First Printing, 1976
Second Printing, 1977

*We dedicate this book to American Indian basketmakers,
past and present. Beautiful examples of their art have inspired us
and given us a greater appreciation of the natural
environments that yield basketry materials.*

ACKNOWLEDGMENTS

We want to extend our deepfelt gratitude to Palmy Weigle who gave us her continued support and encouragement throughout this book's progress, and to Carol's mother, Ruth Grant, whose enthusiasm, advice, and encouragement made it possible for us to begin.

We would like to express thanks to our families, and to Mike and Mary Carstanjen, Jean D'Autilia, Irene Miller, and our many friends who encouraged Carol's basket work in its early stages. We also give thanks to John and Cathy McNealy and Mel Bristol, who gave us information and advice concerning some of the plants mentioned in the book; and to Wayne Rundell, a lover of nature and basketmaker who showed us how to make splints from oak and ash logs. We are grateful to Joanie Hammer, who tried out the first step-by-step instructions, to Lyent Russell who shared his love of Indian baskets and his collection with us, and to Pete Corey who was generous with his research on splint basketry. A special thanks to our editor, Jennifer Place, for her patience and skilled assistance in putting this book together.

Contents

WISTERIA PLANTER

This rustic-looking basket by Carol Hart is made entirely with wisteria runners. They have been woven in a simple manner, and the irregularities in the runners contribute to the basket's charm.

Wic ker Basket. y

Wicker is a word of Scandanavian origin meaning small pliant twig or osier. It is kin to the Swedish word *vikker*, which means willow. The earliest wicker-type baskets were most likely crude containers made of twisted roots, runners, vines, shoots, and twigs. Today the word wicker applies to any round, shootlike material used in woven construction. The most common modern materials used in wicker-work are round reed and willow. The available variety of other commercial, wild, and garden materials suggests endless possibilities for variation and elaboration in wicker basketry.

ROUND REEDS

The most suitable material to use when you begin weaving is round reed. It is both commercially available and manageable. You can learn skills and control your techniques more easily with reed than with the more unpredictable and brittle wild materials.

Round reed is made from the rattan palm, a climbing palm with very long tough stems. Rattan grows in tropical forests in the East Indies and elsewhere. It is harvested, cut, and put through machines that produce the round shape. Reeds range in size from 0 (1¼ millimeters) to 12 (⅜″). Sizes 3 to 5 are the most popular for spokes, sizes 0 to 4 for weavers, and sizes 5 to 12 for handles.

Here are step-by-step instructions for preparing round reed for weaving:

1. Soak each one-pound coil for 2 to 5 minutes in lukewarm water.

2. Untie each coil and lay it straight out on a linoleum floor or some other large waterproof surface.

3. Pull one strand at a time from the bundle and coil each separately into loops ½ to 1 foot in diameter. Twist the ends around the loops to secure them.

4. Dry the loops thoroughly to avoid mildew and store them in a cool, dry place. Hot, dry air will cause them to crack.

5. Soak the reed loops in warm water from 2 to 15 minutes just before using them. The length of soaking time depends on the size of the reed.

6. Wrap the reeds in a damp towel and use them as needed for weaving your basket. If the reed dries before you use it you can put it back in the water, but do not soak it any longer than necessary. Excess soaking darkens the reeds and makes them fray.

FIBERS

Fibers are available in great abundance and variety. They can be used to individualize your wicker basketry designs by adding color, texture, and pattern to the basic form. They can be incorporated into the basket with traditional basketry weaves or by using other techniques such as crocheting, wrapping, or macramé, stitchery, knitting, and netting.

Sea grass, a ropelike twisted grass, and fiber rush, a twisted paper cord, are chair seat weaving materials. They are strong and can be used as weavers to create design in a wicker basket. Heavy cord, rope, and Taiwan jute can also replace your weaver reed because these materials are strong enough to hold the

Commercial Materials. *Here are some of the materials available for making wicker baskets. From right to left, starting with the large center coil, they are round reed, 5-ply jute, Hong Kong grass, 3-ply jute, sisal, tarred marlin twine, and packaging jute.*

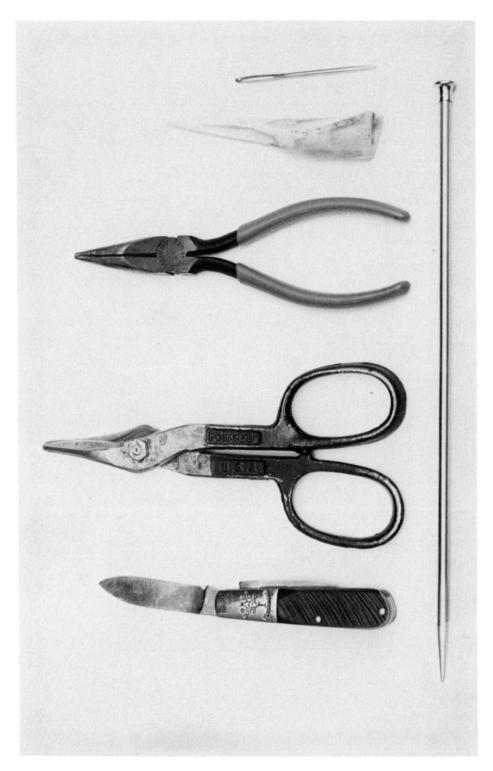

Tools. *The tools used in making wicker baskets include a jackknife, needle-nosed pliers, needle-nosed wire clippers, a bone awl or knitting needle, and a large darning needle.*

shape of the basket. Yarn, lightweight jute or sisal, and other soft materials usually need to be used along with reed as "a double weaver" to ensure strength.

Fibers can be used directly off their spools until you finish a desired amount of weaving. Leave the ends of the fibers long enough so that you can pull them along a spoke in the basket with a crochet hook or darning needle to conceal them. Most fibrous materials will swell, unravel, or become messy if soaked so care should be taken not to get them wet.

TOOLS AND EQUIPMENT

Here are the items you will need to prepare materials for basketmaking:

Soaking pan. This can be any pan with a diameter of at least a foot. A plastic dishpan would be ideal.

Towel. A bath towel should be sufficient.

Jackknife. This is used for cutting and trimming materials.

Needle-nosed Wire Clippers. Tapered clippers are easily maneuvered and strong enough to cut the various sizes of reed.

Needle-nosed Pliers. Pliers are used to pinch and flatten the reed before it is bent. If the reed is not pinched it may resist bending or even break.

Bone Awl or Knitting Needle. Both of these are used to press rows of weaving close together. A bone awl can be made by drying a shin or thigh bone of beef, lamb, or ham. You then smash the bone and file an appropriate piece into the tapered awl shape. A good bone awl is sturdier than a knitting needle.

Crochet Hook and Large Darning Needle. The crochet hook and darning needle are used to secure the ends of fibers into the structure of the basket, as well as to ornament the exterior of the basket with crochet and stitchery techniques.

Measuring Tape. This is helpful when measuring specific lengths of reed.

Glycerin. Add a teaspoon to each quart of soaking water to prevent the reed from fraying.

WILD AND GARDEN MATERIALS

Every region in the world inhabited by man offers plant materials that are suitable for basketry. With the commercialization of a few of these materials, however, the knowledge and use of hundreds of others diminished. An exploration of gardens, fields, pond and stream edges, marshes, and wooded areas should yield many plant materials that can be incorporated into wicker basketry.

Roots, barks, shoots, vines, runners, leaves, and grasses are all possibilities. If a green material can be wrapped around your finger without breaking, you usually can use it for tight weaves such as in the base of a basket. If you can bend the material around your wrist or in a semicircle it may be used in the sides of the basket where stress is not so great. Materials can be gathered without harming the plant. Some may be thinned or pruned. Roots can be gathered where they are exposed on the sides of stream beds or embankments. Bark may be taken off dead or dying trees and vines.

Wild and garden materials give texture, color, and scent to a basket. The following materials are a sampling of those that can be used with success. The creative basketmaker will discover many others to add to this list.

Weeping Willow Branches. The weeping willow (*Salix babylonica*) is a native of China and grows from 30 to 70 feet tall. Its branches are abundantly shed in wind or storms, and because willow trees often need pruning, a plentiful supply is always available. The branches are easy to work into a wicker basket. They are supple and the color — whether green, yellow, or brown — has a rustic quality that is pleasing to look at. The thinner branches are easiest to work with, but they become brittle and fragile when dry and are best used for small weed or dry-flower holders or decoration in a basket made of round reed.

Wash or dip your willow baskets periodically in warm water. This keeps them from getting too dry and brings out the pleasing colors and scent of this material.

Here is the step-by-step procedure for preparing weeping willow branches:

1. Collect and sort the branches according to size.

2. Use the branches green. Store them in a paper bag in a cool, dry place or wrap them in a damp towel and keep them damp for from several days to several weeks. The longer they remain damp the darker they become. Remove branches at different stages of color change. The bark will turn from bright yellow to tan, dark brown, and then black. The process of decay may be faster during the warm months.

3. Soak the dried branches in lukewarm water for a half hour to an hour or until they are flexible. Soak only as many branches as you think you will be using at one time.

Honeysuckle. Japanese honeysuckle (*Lonicera japonica*) is a cultivated plant that escaped and now grows on fences, trees, along roadsides, and at the edge of wooded areas in most of the eastern United States. It can be harvested any time of year but the best time is between September and April. The vines most suitable for weaving are one or two years old and grow along the ground in long, straight lengths.

Honeysuckle vines have a hole running through them. The older vines should be checked because if the hole is larger than half the diameter of the vine it may either split or flatten when used. Use honeysuckle in small baskets.

Here is the step-by-step procedure for preparing honeysuckle:

1. Cut the vine off near the root.

2. Lay the vines lengthwise in bundles that can be tied, looped, and easily carried.

3. Cut off the small branches and leaves. The vines can be used at this stage for a rustic look. The bark is brittle and may break, but the inner vine should not.

4. Coil the vines, place them in a deep pan, and cover them with water. Gently

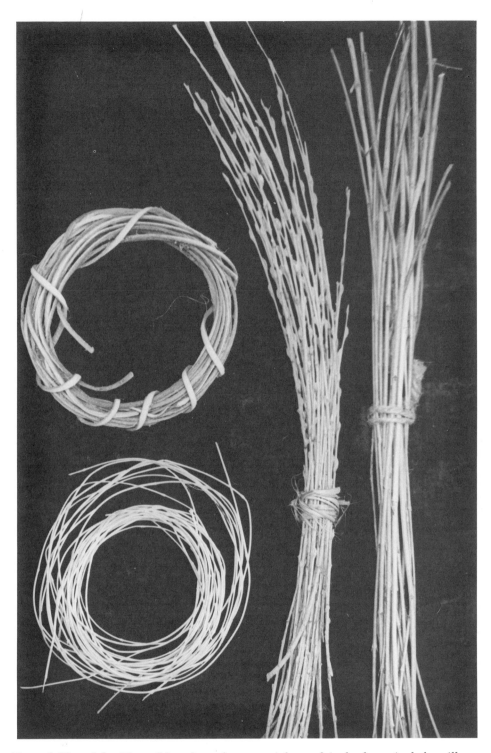

Natural Materials. *The wild and garden materials used in basketry include willow shoots and branches, wisteria runners, and honeysuckle.*

Preparing Cattails

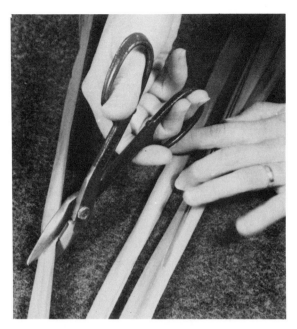

1. *Cut the cattail plant at the base with your jackknife. Then tie the plants in bundles for carrying.*

2. *Separate the leaves and stalks. Trim off the jelly-coated base of the leaves.*

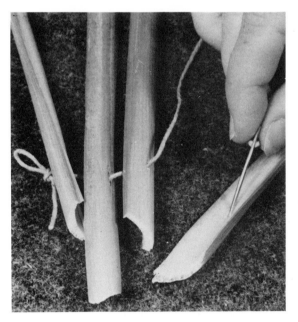

3. *Stitch the base ends of the cattails together with a heavy-duty needle and cord. Hang the leaves in a cool, airy place to store them.*

4. *Soak the cattails in warm water for 20 minutes just before using them. These are soaking in a gutter drain (either line it with plastic or glue on the end pieces with epoxy). Towel-dry the leaves so they are not dripping wet, and keep them wrapped in a damp towel until you need them.*

boil them for about 3 hours until the bark begins to loosen.

5. Rub the vines lengthwise with a cloth to slip off the bark.

6. Trim off the buds, knots, and uneven joints with a jackknife. Coil the honeysuckle vines in bundles until you are ready to use them. Soak the dried honeysuckle until the vine is flexible (about 5 minutes) before you begin weaving.

7. If the inner part of the vine you have gathered is green instead of white, you may leave the color or remove it with commercial bleach.

Cattails. Cattails are commonly found in marshes and ditches and along the shallows of lakes, ponds, and slow streams. The long, slender leaves often reach a height of 6 to 8 feet by late August or September. This is the time to harvest the plant for basketmaking. The split leaves and sliced stalk material can be used as is or it can be twisted, bound, corded, or braided and used as weavers in wicker baskets.

The directions for preparing cattails are given in the demonstration. Some of the ways cattails can be used include the whole leaf, the leaf sliced widthwise, thin slices lengthwise, whole leaf twisted, bundles of thin slices, thin slices bound, width slices twisted, width slices braided. Use a knife to slice the cattail widthwise, and your thumbnail to slice the thin lengths.

Wisteria Runners. There are both native and cultivated species of wisteria. The Japanese *(W. floribunda)* and Chinese *(W. chinensis)* varieties are the ones usually seen covering porches and trellises and are native to the woods and stream banks of those countries. Native or escaped plants can be found running along the ground or climbing trees at the edge of wooded areas. The most suitable parts of the plant for basketry are the long, straight runners that stretch across the top of the ground. These can reach lengths of 12 feet or more. The thicker sizes can be used for spokes, the smaller ones for weavers. The best time to harvest wisteria is in the fall or early spring, but they can be gathered any time of year.

Here is the step-by-step procedure for preparing wisteria:

1. Pull each runner up until you reach the main root. Clip each vine at the root, break off the leaves, and lay the vines lengthwise in a pile. Tie the pile together in several places and loop it for easy carrying. Large runnerlike roots that grow above ground can be clipped and used for handles. This does not kill the plant because the vines keep rooting themselves.

2. You can use the runners right away or hang them to dry in a cool, dry place. If you weave a basket with the green vines the weave will loosen as the vines dry and shrink. Usually this loose-woven look does not detract from the charm of the basket.

3. You can split the runners by inserting the blade of your jackknife through the middle of the clipped end. Hold the runner between the fingers of each hand and open the split with your thumbs. Pull the two halves apart evenly so the split proceeds down the center of the runner. If the split starts to run off to one side you should hold that side of the vine and pull on the other until the split is centered again.

4. Soak the dried runners in warm water overnight, or until they are pliable and ready to use.

DYES

Dyed natural materials can be worked into many interesting patterns and designs that will enhance the charm of a finished basket. Dyes for basketry have been made from roots, barks, leaves, hulls, flowers, fruits, stems, seeds, and complete plants as well as from mud, clays, and rusty nails. Natural colors are more pleasing and complementary to basketry than the harsh hues of aniline dyes.

Keep several things in mind as you prepare your dyebaths. Fresh plant materials seem to yield better color than old or dried ones. The more pulverized the dyestuff, the more efficiently the color can be extracted. Soaking the dyestuff overnight or longer is recommended, especially with woody materials such as barks, hulls, and stems. The more concentrated the dye, the stronger the color will be. If you want stronger colors you can add more dyestuff to the suggested recipe or allow the solution to boil down. The demonstration is for dyeing round reed, but honeysuckle and cattail can also be used.

Here is the equipment you'll need:

Large Enamel Pans. The pans will be used for the dyebaths.

Wooden Spoons. These are used for stirring and turning the dyestuff and the material to be dyed.

Cheesecloth. The cheesecloth is for straining vegetable matter out of the dye.

Rubber Gloves. Gloves help protect the hands from stains.

Clothesline. This should be strung in an airy place so you can hang the dyed basketry materials to dry.

Scale. The scale should measure in ounces and pounds.

Calgon or Rainwater. Dyes work best when prepared with soft water.

The following will give you instructions for preparing dyebaths for both commercial and natural dyes:

Commercial Dyes. Fabric and batik dyes can be used to dye basketry materials when natural dyestuffs cannot be obtained. Follow the directions on the package for dyeing a pound of material.

Black Walnut and Butternut Hulls. Gather the nuts in the fall right after they have fallen off the trees. If the nuts remain on the ground through the winter most of the colorant will leach out of them. Remove the hulls by pounding the nuts with a hammer or by cutting the hulls off with a sharp knife. Wear rubber gloves to protect your hands from being stained. Use the hulls right away or prepare them for storing by spreading them out on a piece of newspaper. To prevent molding, turn them each day until they are dry. Store them in a glass jar.

Dyestuffs. *Dyeing materials used in basketry include black walnuts, butternuts, onion skins, and barberry stems.*

Dyeing Reed

1. Bring the dyebath to a simmer. Coil the reed loosely and immerse it in warm water for 8 to 10 minutes. Shake the excess water from the reed and then put it in the simmering dyebath.

2. Simmer the dyebath for 15 minutes, then remove it from the heat (too much heat makes the reed fibrous). Leave the reed soaking in the bath for 5 minutes to 8 hours depending on the strength of the dye and the color desired. Stir the reed to ensure even dyeing.

3. Rinse the dyed reed with cold water, then hang the reed to dry on a clothesline or in some other airy location.

Put 1½ quarts of dried hulls in an enamel pan. Cover with 6 quarts of water and let them soak overnight or for several days. Bring this dyebath to a boil and boil for an hour. Simmer for 2 more hours, replenishing the water from time to time. Pour the dye solution through cheesecloth into another enamel pan. Repeat so the solution is strained twice.

Both walnut hulls and butternut hulls will give a brown dye. If the butternut dye is allowed to age for several months it will yield grays and blacks depending on its strength. Both dyes can be stored for long periods of time in lidded jars in a cool place. If mold occurs, lift it off the surface of the dye and bring the dye to a boil before using.

Yellow Onion Skins. These are the papery exterior skins of Spanish or Bermuda onions. To significantly dye the woody basketry materials you will need a good quantity of these skins. For 1 pound of reed you should use at least half a grocery bag full of onion skins. Cover the onion skins with water. Simmer the skins for one hour and pour the dye through cheesecloth. For a darker dye the skins may be left to soak in the dyebath overnight, reboiled, and then removed. This dye gives a rusty brown color.

Barberry Stems. Barberry *(Berberis vulgaris)* is a shrub that was imported to this country from Europe and used for hedges. Now you can find barberry running wild throughout southeastern New England in pastures and on sterile or sandy soil. The stems are armed with three-pronged spines so you should wear heavy gloves and use long-handled clippers when gathering them. Barberry root is also a good source of dye.

You can collect barberry stems any time of year. Measure out 10 ounces of larger stems. Shave the bark off the stems with a sharp knife. Split the stems in half lengthwise and then cut them into pieces with clippers. Put the bark shavings and stem pieces into an enamel pan and add a gallon of water. Let this soak overnight. Boil the stems for an hour, then pour the liquid through cheesecloth twice. This solution yields a bright green-yellow dye. For a clear yellow, leave the bark shavings out of the dye.

GLOSSARY

The following terms will help you to understand the step-by-step directions in the following projects for making wicker baskets:

Base. The foot or bottom of the basket on which the basket sits.

Basket Body. The vertical form of the basket from the base to the border.

Border. The finished rim of a basket formed by the spokes.

Spokes. The ribs or framework of the basket. Spokes may form the framework of the base and the side. *Base spokes* refer to those specifically used in the base of the basket. *Side spokes* are those specifically used in the sides of a basket. The *initial spoke* is the first spoke behind which the first weaver is placed. The *odd spoke* is the spoke added as the weaving begins, making the total number of spokes the odd number necessary for a weave.

Stroke. A stitch or movement of the weaver between two spokes.

Weavers. The reed or reeds or other materials woven over and under the spokes.

Onion Basket. *This basket by Carol Hart is made with round reed, onion skins and walnut hull dyes.*

Broombeard Basket. *this basket by Carol Hart is made of broombeard grass dyed with walnut hull and onion skin dyes.*

Wicker Basket. *This smooth, round basket by Carol Hart is made with round reed and 5-ply Taiwan jute.*

Project One

Simple Wicker Basket

This basket demonstrates using continuous spokes in a small, simple basket. You will add an odd spoke to create a warp for three characteristic weaves used with an odd number of spokes: "wicker weave" (over-1, under-1, over-1); twinning (or pairing) using 2 weavers; and twilling (over-2, under-2, over-2). A basic beginning and border are also introduced.

MATERIALS

10 size 3 spokes cut 28″ long.
1 size 3 spoke cut 14″ long.
3 size 1 weavers.
15 (approx.) size 3 weavers.
Tin snips.
Knitting needle.

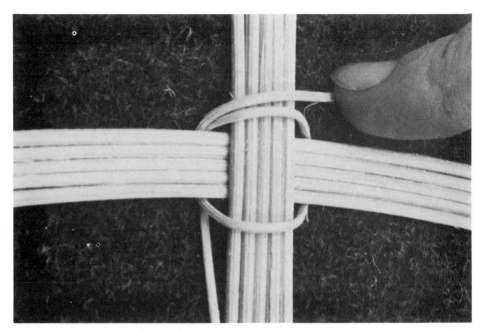

1. Arrange 10 long spokes in a cross as shown. Place the end of a weaver under the left-hand horizontal spokes. Bring the weaver clockwise over the second group of spokes, under the third, and over the fourth. To work the second round, weave over the tail of the weaver before going under the left-hand horizontal spokes again. Then continue weaving over and under.

2. After completing 4 rounds, begin to separate the groups of spokes into pairs. Weave over-2, under-2 for a complete round. Try to keep the spokes equidistant at all times—otherwise the weaving will become cramped in some places and loose in others.

3. You must now add an odd spoke to create an alternately-woven pattern in subsequent rows (otherwise the weaver would continue under and over the same spokes). Push open a hole near the center of the round as shown.

4. Push the end of the odd spoke through the hole and under the left-hand spokes. Then push the odd spoke back up so its end protrudes as shown. Clip off the ends of the tails of both the weaver and the odd spoke. Continue weaving over and under pairs of spokes, treating the odd spoke as if it were a pair.

5. *When the first weaver runs out, introduce a new one by overlapping it next to the end of the old one. Hold both the ends of the old weaver and the new one together until you have completed a round of weaving. Then clip the ends of the weavers so they rest on adjacent spokes and blend inconspicuously into the weave.*

6. *Continue weaving, keeping the tension on the weaver even and bringing the weaver tight against the previous row. Shape the base of the basket as you weave by pressing the spokes forward against your thumb. The finished base should be shaped like a shallow saucer and should be 3½" in diameter. To keep the weave tight without pulling on the weaver, guide the weaver with your forefinger as shown.*

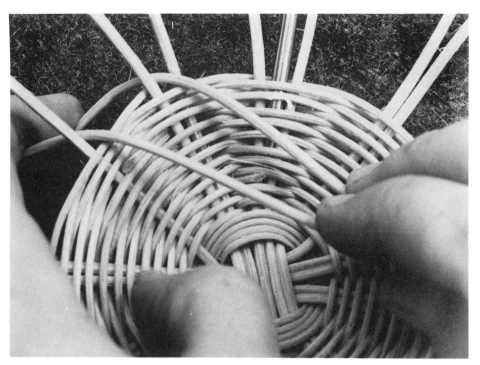

7. *When the base is complete, start to separate the pairs of spokes by wedging a knitting needle between them. Now place the ends of 2 size 3 weavers behind two consecutive spokes, beginning with the odd spoke. Hold the ends as shown.*

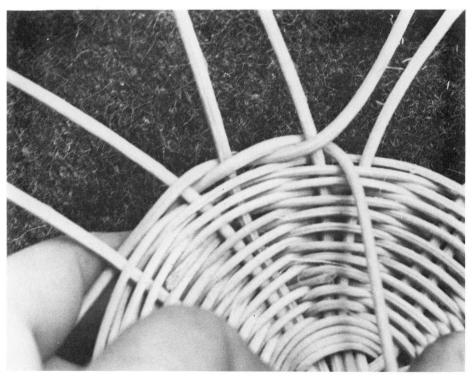

8. *Begin twining with the weaver on the left and weave over-1, under-1. Alternate the position of the weavers and twine them around each spoke as shown.*

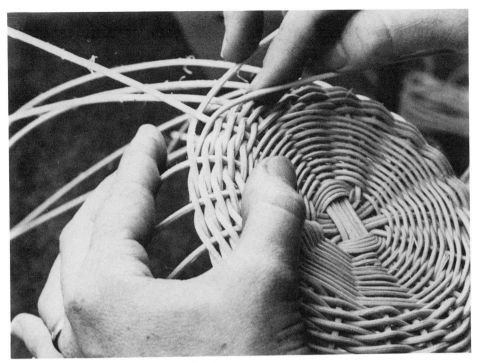

9. *Twine 2 rounds and then begin shaping the turn of the basket by holding the spokes away from you as you weave. Then twine 13 more rounds.*

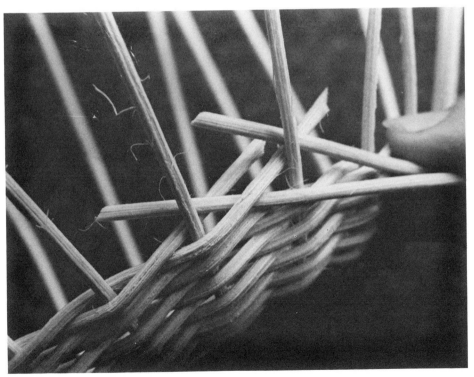

10. *Add new weavers into the twining as shown. Weave two rounds with the new weaver then clip the ends on the inside of the basket while they are still easy to reach.*

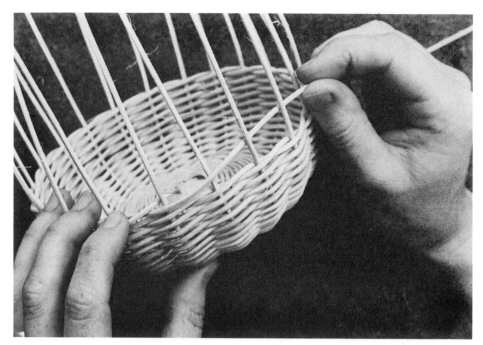

11. *Change the pattern to a twill by clipping off one of the weavers at the odd spoke. Continue weaving over-2, under-2, for 29 rounds. The fingers of the left hand are placed through the spokes once the basket is turned and in a vertical position.*

12. *Add a second weaver at the odd spoke and twine 7 more rounds. End at the odd spoke (there should be at least 6" of spoke length remaining to use for the border). Begin the border by weaving over-2, under-2, over-2 and then dropping the end of the spoke on the inside of the basket. Repeat this process from left to right with each spoke.*

13. *Weave the last five spokes in the same manner. If the border here does not look right, inspect the pattern of the completed border. Each spoke lies on top of the previously woven spoke ends on the bottom inside of the border. Clip off long ends of spokes after the border is complete.*

14. *All your completed planter needs now is an equally beautiful plant.*

Project Two

Jar-Shaped Basket with Lid

This basket has separate base and side spokes. It is a stronger, larger basket than the basket in Project 1. There are an even number of spokes. The weaves used in this basket are the Japanese weave (over-2, under-1); the triple weave (3 weavers, each over-2, under-1); and the quadruple coil (4 weavers, each over-3, under-1).

BASKET MATERIALS

8 size 5 spokes cut 6″ long.

32 size 3 spokes cut 15″ long.

3 size 1 weavers.

30 (approx.) size 2 weavers.

8 size 2 colored weavers.

Tin snips.

Knitting needle.

Pliers.

LID MATERIALS

8 size 5 spokes cut 5½″ long.

32 size 2 spokes cut 6½″ long.

4 size 1 weavers.

10 size 2 weavers.

1. *Arrange 8 short spokes in a cross and bind them as in Project 1, Step 1. Begin the Japanese weave on the 5th round, weaving over-2, under-1. Separate the spokes from one another so they radiate from the center like spokes in a wheel.*

2. *Complete the base (3" diameter) in Japanese weave. Remember to shape it like a saucer. End the weaver by pinching it with pliers and pushing it down into the weave next to the initial spoke.*

3. *Clip a base spoke as close to the weave as possible. Poke the knitting needle down along one side of the spoke to open up the space. Then trim the end of a side spoke at an angle, and insert it into the opened space. Repeat this on the other side of the short spoke. Repeat this process for each spoke in the base.*

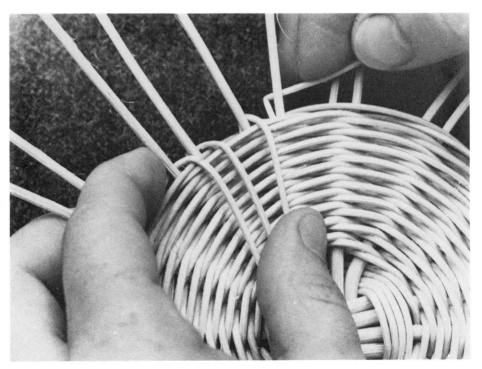

4. *Begin the 4-rod coil by placing 4 weavers side by side as shown. The first weaver should be leaning against the initial spoke. Secure the weavers by pinching the ends and sticking them into the holes at the left side of each spoke.*

5. *Take the left weaver and cross over the other three and behind the spoke directly to the right. After each stroke bring the weaver back to the front so all 4 weavers lie parallel in front of the base. Then make the next stroke. Notice the coil that develops as you weave.*

6. *Weave 2 rounds of 4-rod coiling flat on the base and 2 more rounds as you turn the sides of the basket. When you reach the initial spoke, clip one of the weavers off at an angle as shown.*

7. *Using the remaining 3 weavers, continue in triple weave (over-2, under-1) as shown for 1½".*

8. *Clip a weaver as in Step 6. Trim the end of a colored weaver at a sharp angle and insert it over the clipped weaver. Then wedge its sharp end behind a spoke to secure it.*

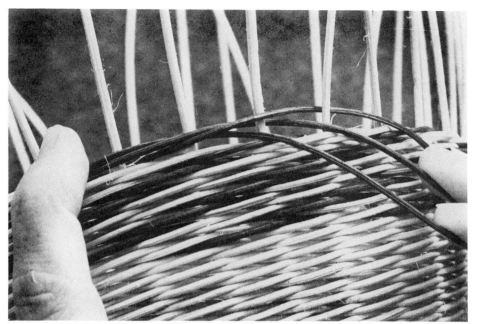

9. *Weave in triple weave for 1½". You should have a pattern of diagonal stripes. Replace the white weavers with two more colored ones and weave about 1" of solid color. Replace two colored weavers with white weavers and weave for 1½". Replace the last colored weaver with a white one and begin pushing in on the spokes to narrow the opening at the top of the basket. Weave in this manner for 3".*

10. *Change the direction of the shape now by pulling the spokes toward you so they stand in a vertical position as you weave the neck of the jar. Insert a 4th weaver and weave 6 rounds of 4-rod coiling. End the weaving at the initial spoke and clip each of the weavers behind consecutive spokes. They should rest against the spokes. The ends can be pinched and inserted next to the spokes as in Step 2.*

11. Begin the border by taking a spoke to the left of a clipped end and weaving it behind the spoke on its right. Do this all the way around. All spokes should be on the outside of the basket.

12. Take any spoke, count 3 spokes to its right, and push it through the hole into the basket. Repeat this procedure, weaving from left to right around the basket. Each stroke begins with the spoke to the right of the one just woven.

13. *Weave the last few spokes carefully. Pull the ends to make sure the border is snug and then clip them close to the weave. Each end should lie against a vertical spoke.*

14. *Begin the lid as you began the basket (Steps 1 and 2). Remember to weave this flat rather than saucer shaped. Add the size 2 side spokes as in Step 3. The smaller size spokes are used here to provide a less conspicuous border. Add the weavers as in Step 4. Use the triple weave rather than the 4-rod coil, and weave just to the edge of the basket border (about 6 rounds).*

15. *Gently pinch the spokes at the edge of the weaving with pliers. Bend the spokes at a sharp angle away from you and make the turn of the basket lid in triple weave. Make your turn as sharp as necessary for a tight fit. Weave ½" and fit the lid to the top of the basket. If the weave is too loose or too tight, take it out and weave it again, adjusting pressure on the spokes accordingly.*

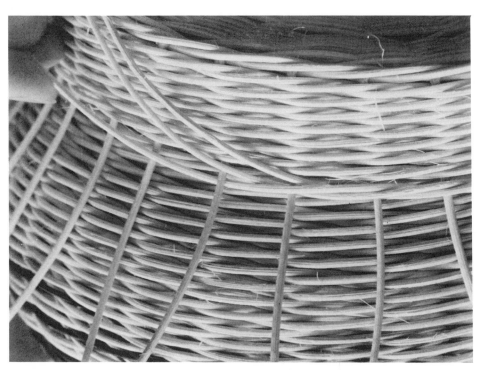

16. *When you are sure the fit is tight at the turn, leave the lid on and weave with the basket upside down for another ½" or so. The sides of your lid should follow the lines of the neck of the basket.*

17. *Finish the lid border as in Steps 10, 11, and 12 of the basket.*

UTILITY BASKET

This simple, squarish basket by Wayne Rundell uses two widths of white oak splints to achieve its pattern. Notice also the open, decorative effect of the border bindings.

Splint Basketry

A splint is a thin, flexible strip of wood used in basketmaking. *Baskawd*, a Welsh word for basket, means woven splinters and is an appropriate description of a splint basket. Originally, all such baskets were made by splitting or pounding logs into long, narrow strips. It is likely that the first settlers in this country were familiar with baskets made of wooden strips. Splint baskets were made and used by the Indians of northeastern North America in harvesting and preparing corn and for storage. The Shakers, known for the quality and grace of their splint baskets, learned the basic techniques of the craft from the Indians. There are many styles of splint utility and sewing baskets. Splint baskets have also been designed to carry such items as wood, wool, cheese, fruit, eggs, produce, oysters, fish, geese, pigeons, and infants.

Splint baskets can be made from commercially available materials such as machine-cut ash, flat reed, flat-oval reed, and cane. They can also be made from barks and strips of wood split or pulled from white oak, ash, and other trees. Splints of wood can be dyed and decorated in a traditional or contemporary manner.

MACHINE-CUT WHITE ASH SPLINTS

These splints are made commercially for weaving chair seats. They are good for the beginner to use to learn technique, but are not the best quality splint for basketmaking. When these splints are prepared, the saw cuts across the annual rings, and therefore they do not have the same flexibility and strength as splints made of the annual rings stripped or split from the logs. The white ash splints may be purchased in 1-pound bundles of 15 strands each, ⅝″ wide and 6 feet long. If this size splint is out of stock a good substitute is ½″ flat reed. A basket may be made entirely of ash splints or the splints can be combined with reed and cane.

Here are the step-by-step instructions for preparing machine-cut ash splints for weaving:

1. Coil the splints and soak them for 5 minutes in warm water and glycerin.

2. Cut the splints into the required lengths for the basket you will be making. It is easier to cut the splints when they are damp, and there will also be less splintering.

3. Hold a splint horizontally at eye level and bend the ends downward so the splint is shaped like a horseshoe. If splintering occurs on the upward side of the splint, then that is the side we will refer to as the rough side. If there is no splintering, then we will refer to the upward side as the smooth side. Each splint has both a rough and smooth side. With machine-cut splints, it is important to arrange your splints so all the rough sides will be on the inside of the basket.

4. The splints should not be soaked longer than the time necessary to soften them. Wrap the splints in a damp towel to keep them damp while weaving the basket.

Knitting Basket. *This 10" high utilitarian basket by Carol Hart is made from white ash and 5mm-wide binding cane. The ends of the different colored yarns stored inside are separated by pulling them through the loops on either side of the basket.*

FLAT REED

Flat reed is the same material as round reed but it is cut into flat strips and resembles white ash splint. It is more flexible than ash splint and the strands are longer. It can be used for both spokes and weavers (the ½″ size is used for spokes in most cases). Flat reed is sold by the pound and can be purchased in 3 sizes: ¼″, ⅜″, and ½″.

Flat-Oval Reed. Flat-oval reed is another product of the inner core of the rattan palm stalk. This reed is flat on one side and rounded on the other. It can be used for spokes if doubled side by side but it is most successful when used as a weaver. The structure of this material seems to make some basket shapes possible that are difficult to accomplish with a flat weaver. Flat-oval reed is sold by the pound in two sizes: ¼″ narrow flat-oval and ⅜″ wide flat-oval.

Here are the step-by-step instructions for preparing flat reed and flat-oval reed for weaving:

1. Soak the reeds for 5 minutes in glycerin and warm water and wrap them in a damp towel.

2. Check each reed splint for its smooth and rough side. This is harder to determine than with ash, but there is a difference. The smooth side should be on the outside of the basket. The oval side of the flat-oval reed will be on the outside.

3. Use the precut sizes of both reeds rather than attempting to cut them into smaller widths. When the reeds are cut, a rough, fibrous edge results.

4. Spoke reeds can be allowed to dry out after the turn of the basket at the base has been made. The dry spokes will give more support to the weaving. Wet the spokes again before turning them at the border.

5. Use ash spokes with reed weavers for larger baskets.

CANE

When the rattan palm is harvested the exterior or surface bark of the stem is removed and marketed as "cane." It has a natural glazed or glossy surface. Cane makes a good weaver and offers the same advantage as flat-oval reed when you shape a basket. It may be used for both spokes and weavers, but the slipperiness of its surface can make this combination tricky to work with. Cane is sold by the bunch. Binding cane comes in 500-foot bunches and three sizes: narrow (4mm) and wide (5mm and 6mm). Natural strand cane comes in 1,000-foot bunches and in 6 sizes. The two sizes most used for basketry are common (3½mm) and medium (3mm).

Here are the step-by-step instructions for preparing cane for weaving:

1. Soak the cane in warm water for 5 minutes, then wrap it in a damp towel.

2. Cut the cane lengthwise if you need a narrower strip, or use a narrower size.

NATIVE BARKS AND WOODS

You will find splint baskets at their best when the materials used are traditionally split or peeled from the trunks and barks of trees. Trees that have been used for making splints are black and white ash, white oak, basket oak, white maple (swamp maple), northern white cedar, buckeye, hickory, poplar, elm, box elder, birch, and cypress. Barks used for making splints include birch bark, elm bark, smooth willow bark, smooth basswood bark, inner bark of hickory, inner bark of white pine, and inner bark of hemlock (spruce pine).

The most widely used trees in the northeast for splints are black and white ash and white oak. White oak, hickory, and ash are used for rim hoops and handles. The inner bark of hickory, thin white oak, or ash splints are used as binding materials when lashing rim hoops to baskets.

To prepare barks and logs for splints you will need a lot of space. An open area outdoors with a pond nearby is ideal. Here is a list of the equipment you will need:

An Axe and a Hatchet.

A Piece of Leather. This should be large enough to cover your knee and thigh.

A Sharp Jackknife and a Whetstone.

A Large Wooden Mallet or Maul. This preferably have a long handle and be made of elm or some other hard, heavy wood. You could also use the blunt, worn backside of an axehead (if the axehead has sharp edges it will break the wood).

Metal and Wooden Wedges. You will need a variety of sizes from 2½″ to 9½″.

A Drawknife. This is to shave the bark off the log and to finish the splints.

Heavy-duty Shears or Tin Snips.

Ash Black ash *(Fraxinus nigra)* also called hoop, basket, brown, swamp, or water ash, is the most northerly of all ashes and ranges from Newfoundland to Manitoba, south to Delaware, Virginia, and Iowa. It is found in wet places such as low woods, cold swamps, or river bottoms that are periodically inundated. The wood of black ash is a beautiful light brown color.

White ash *(Fraxinus americana)*, also called american, biltmore, or cane ash, ranges from Nova Scotia and southern Quebec south to Florida and Texas and west to Minnesota. White ash prefers deep, rich, well-drained to moist soils. It is commonly found in bottomlands, but also ascends slopes where they are not too dry and stony. It can often be found in farmer's woodlots and is a common second-growth tree. The sapwood of the white ash is a yellowish white with pale brown annual growth layers.

Both these ashes have the capacity for splitting easily into thin yet tough pieces. The springwood (the part of the annual growth ring laid down in the spring months when water and sap are plentiful and growth is fast) is made up of large pores with little wood fiber between them. This layer then is almost entirely air spaces. By vigorously beating the ash logs, the springwood is broken down and long strips of tough summer wood can be peeled off.

The step-by-step instructions for preparing ash splints for weaving are given in the demonstration. Other woods from which splints can be made in this manner are sassafras, black elm, white maple, swamp maple, northern white cedar, and poplar. You should soak splints just before using them, and they should be stored in a cool, dry place.

White Ash Splints

1. Find a straight tree 7" to 9" in diameter. Check the bark to make sure there are no twists, knots, or limbs for at least 6 feet. Cut the tree about 8" to 10" above the ground. Once the tree is felled, cut the trunk into a log 6 feet or longer and soak the log in a pond for a month or more.

2. *Use a drawknife and shave all the bark off the log. The layer of bark under the surface will be pithy and fibrous. When you have shaved down to a slick, slippery surface, you have reached the sapwood. Be careful not to shave into it.*

3. *Strike the end of the log diagonally several times as shown. This separates the layers so you can see them.*

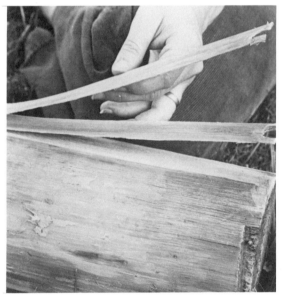

4. *Begin pounding at one end, moving down the log in a straight line. Try to place each swing directly next to the last one. Swing rhythmically and the pounding will be less tiring. Come back up the log, pounding over the same area. Pound the next strip in the same way.*

5. *Pull up 2 or 3 layers of strips at the butt end of the log and peel them off. You may find that scoring each side of the strip with a knife or chisel makes peeling easier. If the strip refuses to peel, then go back to pounding. Peel only as much as you will need, then return the log to the pond to soak.*

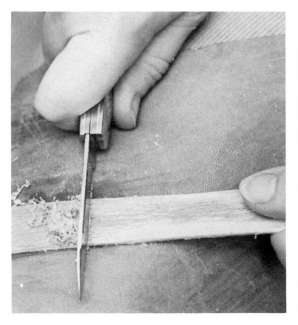

6. *Prepare the splints for weaving while they are still damp. Trim the splints with a knife or shears to widths suitable for spokes and weavers. You can use the splints in this raw state or they can be finished further.*

7. *To finish the splints, place a piece of leather over your thigh. Put the end of the splint on your leg, and holding your jackknife perpendicular to the splint, pull the splint through the "vise", as shown.*

8. *To split the splints into thinner pieces, wedge your knifeblade into the top of a damp splint as shown. Soak the splints before splitting if they have dried out.*

9. *Pull the two halves apart carefully, using your fingers and thumbs as shown. Pull evenly on both sides to make sure the split is centered. After splitting, the splints can be trimmed with scissors.*

Eastern White Oak. Eastern white oak *(Quercus alba)* ranges from Maine and Quebec west to Minnesota, and south to northern Florida and eastern Texas. It is tolerant of most soils except those that are very wet and is found in bottomlands and dry ridges alike. The sapwood is tan to white in color and the heartwood is reddish brown. The wood is very heavy, strong, and close-grained.

Other woods which can be prepared in the same manner as the white oak are hickory and basket oak. Here are the step-by-step instructions for preparing white oak splints for weaving:

1. Find a sapling 4″ to 6″ in diameter. The trunk should be absolutely straight, untwisted, and unmarred by limbs, knots, or imperfections for at least 7 feet. The finer-grained trees seem to grow where there is less sunlight. The lower north slope of a hill, where it is dark and moist, is a good place to start looking. Trees can be taken any time of year, but the best time is late summer or fall.

2. Cut the tree as close to the ground as possible and under the first limb. Section the trunk into 3½- to 7-foot logs to make them easier to carry. It is best to work the log the day it is cut. Otherwise you should keep it soaking.

3. Prop the butt end of the log up on the stump or on another log. Split the end of the log exactly in half using an axe.

4. Open the split by pounding a large wooden wedge into it. Angle the wedge slightly in the direction of the split. Put another wedge in the split created and pound it until the first falls out. Continue leapfrogging the wedges until the log is split. Try to keep the split exactly in the center. If it starts to split off-center, pound a metal wedge in the center of the log to correct the split, or begin splitting exactly in half from the other end. If you are careful, a straight log without knots or branches should not split off-center.

5. Split each half in half following the same procedure. Then split each quarter in half, using smaller wooden wedges.

6. Use a drawknife to shave the bark off of each split section.

7. Split the heartwood off, using the smaller wooden wedges. The heartwood may be knotty. If it is in good condition it can be split and used for rim hoops and handles or accent splints because of its darker reddish color.

8. The pieces of sapwood that you now have are called billets. Use the drawknife to shave the rough edges of the billets and to even up the sides.

9. Begin splitting by pounding the blade of your knife into the center of the billet, parallel with the annual rings. Open up the split, and as soon as you can get your hands between the halves slowly and evenly pull the two pieces apart.

10. If one side of the split begins to run out, pull down harder on the other. If the splints bind as you are splitting, cut them free.

11. Split each of these halves in turn and continue splitting each piece until you reach the thinness desired. Observe the thickness of splints in old baskets to get an idea of how thin yours should be.

12. Finish the splints by shaving them with a drawknife or a jackknife (see Step 9 of how to prepare ash splints).

Basswood Bark. Basswood *(Tilia americana)*, or American linden, whitewood, or bee tree ranges from New Brunswick to Manitoba, south to Delaware and eastern Kansas, and along the Appalachian Mountains to North Carolina. The preferred habitat is bottomland where the soils are deep, moist, and fertile, but basswood is often found on the slopes of hills and even in rocky places. The inner bark yields the longest, toughest fiber in our native flora. It was stripped by Indians in the spring and used to make thread, twine, and rope. The entire bark of the basswood can be used to make splints.

The step-by-step demonstration for preparing basswood bark for weaving is shown nearby. Other trees whose barks can be removed in a similar manner and used for splints are willow, birch, white pine, hemlock, and elm. Try to get young trees with smooth bark, and try to use the splints right away. Soaking these splints will cause sugars and other substances to coat the bark, making it difficult to work with.

DYES

The dyes listed in *Wicker Basketry* may be used with splints as well as reeds. If more solution is needed to cover the splints, you can double or triple the recipes given. The directions for dying splints and cane are the same as for dying reed for wicker. Splints resist dye more than reeds, so it is a safe rule to let them cool and soak overnight in the dyebath. Make sure the splints are loose enough in the dyebath so the solution reaches all parts and dyes evenly.

Following are recipes for black oak and hickory hull dyes. Mordants are used with the black oak bark. A mordant helps to fix the color by enabling it to ''bite'' or combine with the fibers of the material and therefore make the colors fast. Indians and colonial dyers used various plants and household substances for mordants, including wood ashes, salt, urine, rusty nails, vinegar, soda, sorrel, and hemlock. Today salts of aluminum, iron, chromium, and tin are commonly used as mordants. The color varies according to the metal used.

Here is a list of materials you will need for dyeing:

Calgon. A water softener, which should be used if you have hard water.

Alum (potassium aluminum sulfate). This is added to a dyebath to brighten a color.

Cream of Tartar. Adding this to the dyebath distributes the mordants evenly in the solution.

Tin (stannous chloride). This acts as a brightening or blooming agent for colors. It must be used with care as too much can make the material brittle. It is also poisonous, so keep containers out of the reach of children and prepare it in a well-ventilated area.

Enamel pans. These should be large enough for the splints.

Rubber gloves. These will protect your hands from stains.

Basswood Bark Splints

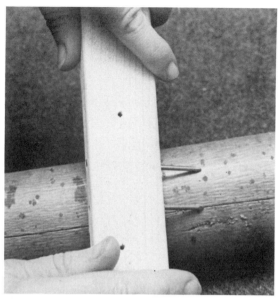

1. *Select a tree 3" to 5" in diameter with very smooth bark. The tree can be felled any time, but spring is best. The bark separates more easily when the sap is running. Slit the trunk in a straight line from end to end. Make the cut deep enough so it cuts through the entire bark layer.*

2. *Make a splint gauge by hammering nails through a small wooden board 1 foot long. Place the nails 1" apart or the desired width of the spokes. These can be cut in half lengthwise for weavers. Draw the gauge down the bark as shown, pressing gently so the bark is not torn. Follow the lines with your knife to cut through the bark layer.*

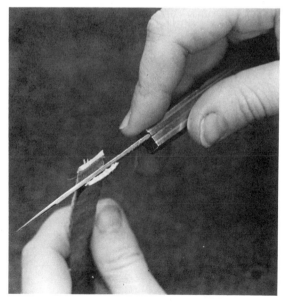

3. *Remove the first strip by prying it away from the sapwood as shown. Pull carefully. If the bark fibers stick you can cut them free with your knife.*

4. *Use the strips whole or separate the inner and outer barks by wedging in the knife blade and pulling them apart. Both the inner and outer bark strips can be used.*

Wooden Spoons. You will need one for each dye.

Measuring Spoons. Use these only for mordants, not for cooking as well.

Scale. This should measure in ounces.

Cheesecloth. This is to strain the dye.

Hickory Hull Dye. Shagbark hickory *(Carya ovata)*, also known as shellbark or scalybark hickory, ranges from southern Maine south along the Piedmont to southern Georgia and to southeastern Texas. It also grows from Ontario through the Great Lakes region, Iowa, Nebraska, Kansas, and Oklahoma. This hickory can easily be identified by its smoke-gray bark that warps away from the trunk in large plates of bark a foot or more long. Gather the hulls in the autumn as they drop from the tree (if hulls sit on the ground for long the colorant leaches out of them).

Crush 2 gallons of hickory hulls. Put them in an enamel pan, cover them with water, and soak them for a week or two. Bring the hulls to a boil and boil for an hour, then simmer for 2 hours. Cover the pan or replenish the water as it evaporates. Let the solution cool and then strain it through cheesecloth. Refer back to the directions for dyeing round reeds if necessary. This dye yields a tan color. Since it is a light color, you may soak the splints and cane for up to two days.

Black Oak Dye. Black oak *(Quercus velutina)*, also known as yellow, dyer's, or quercitron, ranges from southern Maine to southern Michigan, and through parts of Wisconsin, Minnesota, Nebraska, and Kansas, south to western Florida and eastern Texas. Black oak ascends to 4,000 feet in the southern Appalachians. The bark is deeply furrowed and broadly ridged. You can easily tell black oak from other oaks by scratching a twig with your thumbnail; you will find a characteristic yellow or orange color to the inner bark. The dye extracted from this bark is a brilliant yellow and is very effective for dyeing basketry material.

Black oak bark can be collected when a tree has been felled, or you can get the bark from a sawmill. If you go to a sawmill, be sure they give you the bark from the right tree. It can be stored in paper bags in a cool, dry place.

Here are the step-by-step directions for preparing black oak dye:

1. Combine 6 ounces of oak bark (use both the outer and inner bark) with 1 teaspoon cream of tartar, 1¼ teaspoons alum, and 1 teaspoon tin in a gallon of water.

2. Heat and stir until all chemicals dissolve. Bring the mixture to a boil. The color will begin to show in the bath fairly soon.

3. Put in the material to be dyed when the bath is yellow. This bath should be strong enough to dye from ½ to 1 pound of splints.

4. Simmer until the desired color is reached.

5. Let the dyebath cool, but while the bath is still warm remove the dyed material and rinse in mild, soapy water. Then rinse again under the tap until the water runs clear.

Dyestuffs. *Hickory hulls and black oak bark are often used to make dyes for basketry materials.*

DECORATIVE COLORINGS

Many of the northeastern Indians of the Algonquin group stamped, painted, and swabbed their splints to create decorative designs on their baskets. Pigments for this decoration were originally made by pressing ripe berries such as pokeberry, inkberry, or huckleberry, and also by boiling the roots of goldthread, bloodroot butternut, spruce, barberry, and other trees and plants down to the consistency of ink. Liquid bluing, used to brighten laundry, later became a favorite pigment along with indigo red and blue inks, and aniline dyes. You may also want to try batik dyes, India ink, or wood finishes such as Minwax. Splints colored with waterproof dyes or stains can be soaked in warm water before weaving. Your own painted designs and combinations can serve to convey a personal message as well as being decorative.

Stamping. It is believed that the Indians originated the practice of stamping designs on splint baskets. Stamps were made of a variety of materials including carved white cedar, arbor vitae, and basswood; bone; a fingertip; coiled belt leather; a carved potato or turnip; the incised end of a cotton spool; and bundles of matchsticks in a cluster. The softer materials work best on splints. Vegetable stamps only last a short time so you should use them the day you carve them.

Here is the procedure for stamping a basket with a carved stamp:

1. Carve a relief design in a piece of potato, turnip, cork, or eraser with the tip of your jackknife. Make sure the surface is flat before carving.

2. Put each color into a separate saucer. Place a pad of absorbent cloth in the bottom of each saucer. This allows the pigment to spread evenly over the surface of the stamp.

3. Press the carved stamp into the pad and apply it to a piece of paper to see if the impression is clear. Then begin to stamp your basket. You may be able to make several impressions before you have to re-ink the stamp.

4. Keep the dye in saucers if they contain water-soluble pigments. The dye will dry out and can be reconstituted by adding water to the pad. Waterproof pigments should be poured back into their containers and the saucers washed.

Painting. Designs were also painted freehand on baskets after they had been woven. The Mohegans made a brush for basket painting by fraying the end of an alder twig. Use sable or bristle artist's brushes and any of the pigments previously discussed to paint your own designs.

Swabbing. The outer sides of splints were often swabbed with pigment before they were woven. Blues and reds seem to have been the most popular colors.

Here are step-by-step directions for using laundry bluing (Bleachette brand) for coloring splints:

1. Spread newspaper on a table and pour a little bluing into a tunafish can.

2. Put a dry splint, smooth side up, on the newspaper and carefully apply the bluing with a ½″ bristle brush. Make sure the color does not run off and splotch the opposite side of the splint. Apply a second coat if needed.

3. Let the splint dry for about 5 minutes. Although the bluing will now be dry, the splint should still be damp enough to weave easily. You should not soak the splint before using it because the bluing will be wet and the surface is likely to smudge in the process of weaving. For this reason it is important not to prepare blued splints until you are ready to use them.

GLOSSARY

Base-mat. The square or rectangular mat woven for the bottom of the blanket.

Border Lashing. The binding at the border of the basket, usually consisting of a narrow strip of splint wound around the border splints to secure them to the basket.

Checker Weave. This is the over-1, under-1 weave of splint basketry.

Spokes. The upright or vertical splints, often wider than the weavers.

Twill Weave. This is an over-2, under-2 weave.

Weavers. These are the horizontal splints and may vary considerably in width.

Wastebasket. *The two-color effect of this decorative basket by Carol Hart was achieved by dyeing white ash splints with walnut hull dye.*

Basswood Bark Basket. *This simple basket by Carol Hart has a handle made from a pliable shoot that was tied when green in the desired shape.*

Splint Baskets. *These baskets, by Carol Hart, are made from white ash splints and wild grape bark. The use of the grape bark makes a nice pattern in the middle of each basket.*

Project Three

Splint Basket with Round Lid

This is a simple, square-based basket made of white ash and cane. You will have an odd number of spokes and will use an over-under, or checker, weave. The border is held with a crossed lashing. The round lid will give you experience in beginning a round-based basket.

BASKET MATERIALS

12 ash splint spokes 22″ long.
7 (approx.) 5mm cane weavers.
Wire clippers or heavy-duty scissors.
Knitting needle or bone awl.
1 splint to cut for the border.
Ruler.

LID MATERIALS

16 ash splint spokes 15″ long.
3 3mm cane weavers.
2 5mm cane weavers.
Pencil.

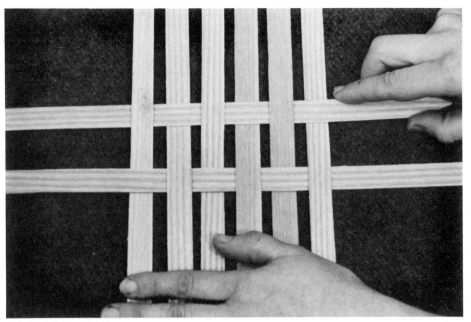

1. Arrange 6 splints so they are parallel, with their smooth sides down. Weave in a splint from the right and place it to the right of center. Weave in 2 more splints from the right and then weave in 3 from the left. Leave space between the splints as shown until they are all woven. Then tighten the weave beginning with the splints in the center. The base mat is complete when the spaces between the spokes are all approximately ¼" and the weave is centered.

2. Soak the base in warm water for 5 minutes. Lay a ruler along each side of the base as shown and push the spokes gently against the edge. This slight bending makes turning the basket easier for the beginner.

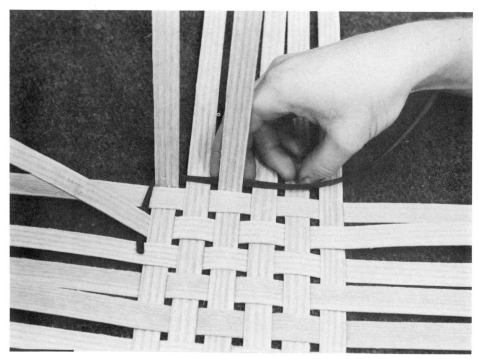

3. Add the first weaver as shown with the glossy side of the cane on the outside. Weave over-1, under-1 all the way around the base. Keep the weaver taut, especially at each corner. The corner spokes should stand up vertically.

4. Cut the initial corner spoke in half with shears where the weaver begins to overlap itself. This gives you the required odd number of spokes. Weave through each half as if it were a separate spoke. Continue weaving over-1, under-1, bringing the second round of the weave down tight against the first.

5. *Pull the spokes apart before weaving the sides of the basket. This increases the space between spokes and makes the basket flair out. Lean your fingers and hands against the spokes as you weave when you want to bring the shape in again.*

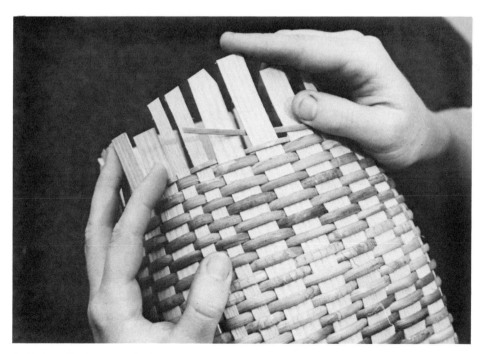

6. *Before the last round of weaving you should taper the weaver so its width diminishes. This should keep the top of the basket from being lopsided. End the weaver behind the initial, or split, spoke. Using your fingers, a knitting needle, or a bone awl, tighten the weave by pressing on the weaver. Begin at the bottom and turn the basket as you go.*

7. *Cut the remaining spokes to 2½" above the weave. Clip the spokes on the inside of the weaver off at the weave. Trim the outside spokes as shown above.*

8. *Lightly score the outside of each remaining spoke just above the weave. Then soak the top of the basket for 5 minutes in warm water.*

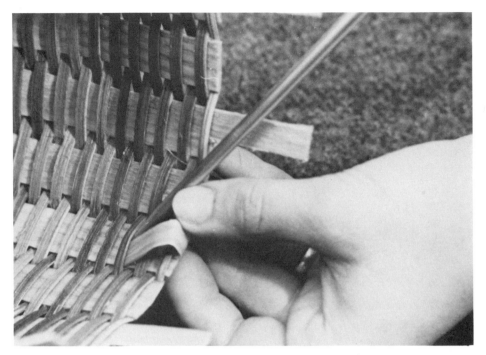

9. *Lift up the third weaver from the top on the inside of the basket with the bone awl or knitting needle and tuck the spoke under it. Do this with each remaining spoke.*

10. *Measure the circumference of the top of the basket and cut 2 splints 1½" longer than that measurement. Then cut each of the 2 splints in half lengthwise. Now you have 4 splints to use in the border. Beginning at the split spoke, thread the binding weaver under the top round of weaving with the shiny side facing down. Use the knitting needle to open a space between the weavers to make threading easier. Lay two of the border splints together with the smooth surfaces facing outward. Arrange these on the inside of the basket border as shown.*

11. *Put the other two border splints together in the same way and lay them on the outside of the basket. Take the long end of the binding weaver and lash it over the splints (make sure you lash only the top row of weaving).*

12. *Overlap the ends of the border splints and lash them together snugly. Then reverse your direction and lash around the border again. Tuck the end of the binding cane into the weaving on the inside of the basket.*

13. *Begin the circular lid by arranging the spokes as shown with the smooth sides up. Weave over-1, under-1, making sure the weaver goes under the spokes on the bottom and over those on top. Pull the weaver tight as you make the round. Split the initial spoke before weaving the second round. After the second round is complete check the weave. If the weaving does not form a circle, tap with the knitting needle until you get the right shape. Weave 7 more rounds.*

14. *Stop weaving the seventh round at the split spoke. The weaver should be behind the first side of the split spoke and in front of the second to ensure that the following weave is correct. Now mark the remaining 8 splints at the edge of the weave as shown (you may mark one and use it as a model for the rest). Then cut them so each splint tapers from the end to the marks.*

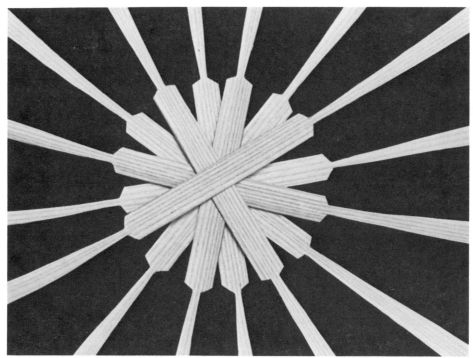

15. *Cross the cut spokes as shown, smooth side up, and lay the base on top of them. Do not place a spoke between the halves of the split one, but arrange them on either side.*

16. *The weaving should now continue under the new spokes, catching and holding them against the base. Keep weaving until the lid reaches the diameter of the top of the basket. Soak the lid in warm water for 5 minutes, then turn the spokes at a sharp enough angle to make a snug fit and weave 3 or 4 rounds with the small weaver. Next taper the end of a 5mm weaver and add it at the split spoke. Weave 5 or 6 rounds. Finish the lid in the same manner as you did the basket.*

17. Here are two variations of the same basket. The basket you just made is on the left. The one on the right includes a twill weave (over-2, under-2). You may want to try varying the style in other ways, using different size cane, splint weavers, increasing the numbers and length of spokes, or embellishing the basket with stitchery, beads, bones, shells, or feathers.

Project Four

Rectangular-Based Basket with Handle

This basket has an even number of splints, a new weaver for each round, trimmed spokes for a greater variation in shape, an alternative method of trimming the rim spokes, and a wrapped handle.

MATERIALS

6 ash splint spokes cut 27″.

10 ash splint spokes cut 25″.

8 5mm cane weavers.

3 ash splints to use for weavers and border.

2 pieces of 5mm cane cut 7″ for loops to hold the handle.

1 size 10 round reed cut 22″ for the handle.

1. *Make the base as in Steps 1 and 2 of Project 3. This base, however, is rectangular and should measure about 9" x 12". Add the weaver as shown in Step 3, Project 3, but have the glossy side of the cane facing the inside of the basket. Keep the weaver tight enough so the corner spokes stand up.*

2. *Overlap the first weaver as shown and clip the end on the inside of the spoke. Push the overlapping end down so it lies directly over the first round. Now add the second weaver to the left of where the first began. The beginning strokes of weaving should hold down the ends of the first round securely. Continue weaving until 3 rounds have been completed.*

3. *Add an ash splint weaver by threading it through the spokes at the top of each side and then pushing down tight against the cane weaving. If the spokes are too close together the splint will not lie tightly into the weave. If this is the case you will need to spread the spokes by pulling them apart. Overlap the ends of the splint for 2 spokes, then clip the weaver on the inside of the 2nd spoke.*

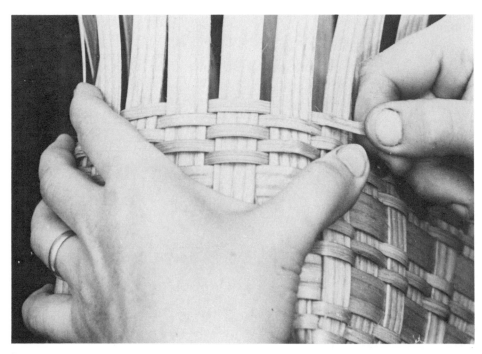

4. *Weave 3 more rounds of cane, 1 round of ash, and then 11 rounds of cane. As you begin the last section of cane, make sure the splints are damp. Then, as you weave, squeeze the ends of the basket as shown and pull the weaver tight. As you push in on the sides, the shape of the basket should start to come in.*

5. *When the splints start to converge, taper them with your shears from the top to the weave as shown. Then continue weaving.*

6. *Add another splint weaver, pushing it down tight against the weave and forcing the direction of the spokes straight up and down. Weave 2 more rounds of cane.*

7. *Prepare the spokes for turning as you did in Project 3. Turning will be easier if you trim the spokes as shown here. Tuck all spoke ends into the weaving.*

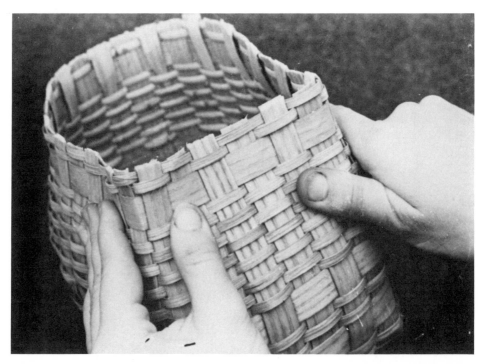

8. *Squeeze the corners at the top of the basket if you would like to have a rectangular shape to your basket. You may prefer to leave it oval-shaped.*

9. *Bind the borders by lashing on splints as you did in Project 3. Have the matte side of the binding cane facing outward. Finish by tucking the end of the cane into the weaving on the inside of the basket.*

10. *Trim the size 10 reed so 3" of each end is tapered. Then trim a strip off either side of the length of the handle as shown.*

11. Take a 7" piece of cane and loop it, glossy side out, around 2 weavers in the center of each side of the basket. Secure the ends by tucking them under weavers on the inside. The ends should overlap each other snugly.

12. Insert the handle through the loop. Begin wrapping the handle by bending the binding cane around the tapered end. Wrap so the end is pulled tightly against the handle. The tail of the cane should be hidden on the inside of the wrapping.

13. Keep the wrapping as tight as possible so the handle is completely covered. Continue wrapping until you reach the other end of the handle. Keep the last two wraps loose enough so that the end of the cane can be pulled through them. Pull until the wrapping is tight and clip off the end.

14. You can make a lid for this basket by following the directions for the base. Use 13" and 17" spokes. Weave 2 rounds of cane, 1 round of ash, 2 more of cane, and then add the same type border as for the basket. Variations of this basket can be made by adding more ash weavers, making the sides straight, varying the number of rounds of cane between the ash weavers, using different colored weavers, and stamping or painting designs on the splints.

LARGE KNITTING BASKET

This basket by Joan Hammer has a rope core and uses jute stitching material. The pattern developes by changing the color of jute with each row—the stitch repeat does the rest.

Coiled Basketry

A coil is a series of connected spirals or rings. You make a coiled basket by winding a series of coils, one on top of another, and wrapping or stitching these coils together as you build. The two structural parts of a coiled basket are called the *core* or foundation material and the *stitching* or sewing material. The core gives the basket its strength, so the material used should be strong yet flexible enough to be bent into coiled forms. It can be made of from 1 to 4 lengths or rods arranged by side by side or grouped, or from a bundle of finer strands. The core is usually hidden under the stitching unless an open stitch is used. The stitching material holds the coils together and gives the basket its color, texture, and surface design.

Coiled baskets made of grasses, split shoots, roots, plant fibers, leaves, and barks have been used throughout history for everything from cooking pots, water containers, and storage and burden baskets to spectacular ceremonial baskets adorned with quail and woodpecker feathers and beads.

ROUND REED

Round reed is a good core material because it is both sturdy and flexible. Use the reed in groups of from 1 to 4 rods or in bundles. Sizes 1 to 3 are preferable for the bundle cores and sizes 3 to 5 for the rod cores. The larger the size of reed, the harder it is to bend it around corners. In some cases you might want to begin your basket with a small size and insert larger sizes as you work. If you have trouble making the bends at the beginning of the basket, try pinching the reed with pliers for the length of the bend. Keep the reed damp while you stitch the base of the basket. Once you begin weaving up the side it is not necessary to keep the reed damp, although it may be helpful. For instructions on preparing the reed see *Wicker Basketry*. Use reed as a core with raffia or wild and garden stitching materials.

FIBER RUSH

Fiber rush is a chair caning material made of twisted paper. It is good to use as a core material. Soaking will cause the rush to swell and untwist, so keep it dry and use it with stitching materials that do not need soaking. Fiber rush is sold by the pound in four sizes. The best sizes for coiled basketry are $^4/_{32}''$ and $^5/_{32}''$.

HONG KONG GRASS

This is a handmade seat weaving material produced in China. It is made of twisted grass in the same manner as rope and makes a good core material for coiled baskets. You do not need to soak Hong Kong grass. It can be used with stitching materials that require soaking as well as with yarns and cords. The size of the grass varies because it is handmade, and it is generally sold in 3-pound coils.

RAFFIA

Raffia is a product of Madagascar. It is made by cutting the palm leaf before it uncurls, stripping the tough underside of the leaf, then drying the strips and splitting them to the desired widths. The strands vary in length and may be as

Commercial Materials. *The materials available for coiled basketry include round reed, raffia, needlepoint yarn, Persian wool, embroidery thread, ribbon, cotton sash cord, braided polypropylene rope, jute, Greek handspun wool, metallic thread, corday, nylon twine, homespun linen, and waxed linen.*

long as 5½ feet. You can use these strands for stitching material or bundle them for the core. Both natural and dyed raffia is sold by the pound.

Here are step-by-step instructions for preparing raffia for weaving:

1. Cut the binding strands around the bundle of raffia and shake the raffia until it hangs loosely from the large binding knot at the top end of the bundle. Hang the bundle from a strong nail.

2. Clip the strands of raffia right under the binding knot so you get the longest pieces possible. Try to choose pieces that are about the same width and thickness.

3. If you are using the raffia for stitching, make a loop of each strand and wrap the end of the strand around the rest of the loop to hold it together. If you are using the raffia for core material, loop the strands in bunches.

4. Add 1 teaspoon of glycerin to 1 quart of warm water and stir. Soak the loops of raffia for 5 or 10 minutes or until they appear transparent.

5. Put the soaked loops in a damp towel and use them as needed.

Basket with lid. *A raffia core and stitching material make up this tightly-stitched basket by Dolly Curtis.*

ROPES, CORDS, AND FIBERS

There are many varieties of ropes, cords, and fibers that can be used for core material. Twisted hemp or sisal are the toughest ropes but are also hard on your hands. Braided cotton clothesline and sash cord and braided polypropylene or nylon rope are strong, easy on your hands, and do not have twists that would be evident through the stitching. A twisted rope is easier to taper at the start and finish of a basket, however, and you may prefer to use it for that reason.

Jute. Jute is available in many sizes and colors. It makes a more flexible core than rope and allows for more fanciful basket forms. Use the larger sizes for core material in the same way as you would rope, and bundle the smaller sizes. Bundled jute is a popular core because several of the strands in the bundle can be separated from the main core and wrapped separately, then incorporated back into the core. The design possibilities of a basket are therefore multiplied.

Yarn. You can use a wide variety of yarns for stitching material. The tighter yarns give more of a grain or texture to the basket than the fluffier, fuzzier yarns. Rya rug yarn, Persian wool, wool twist, tapestry and needlepoint yarns, and many weaving yarns work very well in coiled baskets. Braided nylon rope is a good core material to use with yarns.

Cords and Threads. Cotton, sisal, nylon, corday, and satin cords; linen and waxed linen; crochet and embroidery cotton; weaving threads; and many synthetic fibers all can be used in coiled baskets. Sisal is hard on your hands, but Irish sisal comes in such beautiful colors that you may want to try it. Braided nylon mason line is easier to use than 2-ply nylon mason line, which tangles and twists back on itself as you stitch. Hold a flame briefly to the end of a nylon stitching cord if it begins to unravel as you use it.

Ribbon. Satin and other types of ribbon, strips of upholstery material, thin leather, rawhide, metallic wrapping paper, and other flat materials can be used for imbricating coiled baskets (an additional strip wrapped over the regular stitching to create a decorative effect). The ribbon or strips can be as wide as the coil. The most commonly used widths are ¼″ and ½″.

Brass, Copper, and Metallic Threads. These shiny wires and threads can be used to add highlights and variations to a fiber-stitched basket. You can buy brass, copper, and steel household wire at most hardware stores. They are sold in 1-ounce spools and can be used for stitching and wrapping. Metallic threads are available at fabric and yarn shops and can also be used as stitching materials.

CARE OF FIBER-STITCHED COILED BASKETS

Make sure your hands are clean while you are making your baskets. As soon as you finish baskets stitched with yarns, jutes, linen, cotton, or nylon fibers, spray them with a sealer such as Scotch Guard to protect them from permanently soiling. Once they are sealed they can be more easily cleaned. Remember not to place these baskets in direct sunlight or the colors may fade.

TOOLS AND EQUIPMENT

Here are the things you will need for preparing natural materials:

Long Plastic Tub or Gutter Drain. These are for soaking your natural materials. If you try to bend dry grasses and leaves to fit into a small dishpan, they will break.

Towel.

Knitting Needle or Bone Awl.

Sharp Jackknife.

Scissors and Pruning Shears.

Pliers.

Measuring Tape.

Knitter's "Bone" Rings. These are plastic rings used to keep the size of grass and leaf bundle cores consistent. They come in a variety of sizes.

Glycerin. A teaspoon of glycerin added to each quart of soaking water keeps raffia and other plant materials from becoming brittle. Pre-mordanted and dyed raffia becomes quite brittle. The glycerin-soaking water restores its waxy resiliency.

Large Yarn Needles and Blunt Darning Needles. These should be metal (plastic bends).

WILD AND GARDEN MATERIALS

Some of the native materials that can be used in coiled baskets have already been discussed in previous chapters. Split willow shoots or bundles of weeping willow branches are good to use for core material. Honeysuckle can be used both for core and for stitching material. Wisteria runners and cattail leaves can be used whole or split and bundled for the core, and they are also good stitching materials. Thin ash and oak splints can be used for stitching, especially when you have a thick core.

Grasses. You will find an infinite variety of grasses that can be used for basketry, each with its particular color, scent, tassel, leaf, and stem form. Grasses are distinguished from other plants by hollow stems that are interrupted by nodes, leaves that are long and narrow, and the base of which ensheathes the stem, and flowers that are small and borne in dense spikes or open branching clusters.

Three grasses commonly found in the eastern half of the U.S. that can be used in coiled baskets are tall redtop, broomsedge, and phragmites. Tall redtop *(Triodia flava)*, named for its red to purplish hue, is a tall (2 to 4 feet) native perennial found abundantly covering pastures, roadsides, and fallow fields in the summer and fall. Broombeard *(Andropogon virginicus)* was so named because in the south handsful were used as brooms. It is also a tall (2 to 4 feet) bushy perennial with the upper two-thirds freely branching. It forms solid stands in fallow fields and colors them a reddish brown. Phragmites *(Phragmites communis)*, also called common reed, cane, or feathergrass, is a giant grass that can grow to over 12 feet. It can be found covering poorly drained land, especially around marshes and lakes. In summer and fall a large tawny to purplish plume tops this plant. Gather these plumes in early spring. The winds of a winter have blown most of the fluff out of them leaving the dry, papery bracts. These tassels can be used in the core of a basket where you want texture to show through.

Natural Materials. *Here are some native plant materials. From left to right, they are broombeard grass, soft rush, and Siberian iris leaves.*

Phragmite Tassle. *These phragmite tassles add nice texture to open-stitched coiled baskets.*

Here are the step-by-step instructions for preparing grasses for baskets:

1. Cut the grasses in the late spring, summer, or fall. The same grass will have different qualities with each season. If the grass is green when you cut it, tie the stems in bundles and hang them upside down to dry in a shady, dry place. The grass will retain much of its color. If you cut grass in the fall it will probably be bleached and dry. Stack the grass, tassels up, in paper bags and store in a cool, dry place.

2. Soak the grass for a half hour in cold water (warm water will wash out the color). Wrap the soaked grass in a towel until you need it. In some cases, as with the Phragmites tassels, you will want to use the grass dry rather than soaking it.

3. Hold the grass in bundles as you stitch. You can keep the grass even or twist the bundles, especially if you are using grass stems that tend to bend in angles. If you are using a large bundle of grass, or you would like an aid in keeping the size of the bundle consistent, it is helpful to slip a plastic "bone" ring over the bundle before you begin. Keep the ring just ahead of the stitching. When the grass in the ring starts to get thin or loose, add more grass to the center of the bundle through the ring.

4. If well soaked, the stems of some grasses can be split along one side with your thumbnail, opened up, and used for stitching or imbrication.

Rush. There are many species of rush in the U.S. They are emergent plants with flattened, often hollow leaves and unbranched, cylindrical, hollow or pith-filled stems that end in a spearlike point. The flowers are born in clusters on or near the tip of the stem. They grow in shallow fresh water and salt marshes and in poorly drained meadows and pastures. Rushes can be used both as core and as stitching material in coiled baskets.

One rush that can be easily found in the eastern part of the U.S. and elsewhere is soft rush *(Juncus effusus)*. It grows in dense clumps in open swamps and wetlands. The leaves and stems are dark green and cylindrical, and the stems are filled with a white pith. The flower develops on one side of the stem, near the tip, and looks like a cluster of small brownish capsules.

Here are the instructions for preparing soft rush for baskets:

1. Cut the rush as near to the base of the plant as possible. The best time to cut is late summer when the rushes have reached their maximum height.

2. Dry rush bundles by placing them upright in a large paper bag or hanging small bundles in a shady or cool, dry place. If you hang the rushes you should tighten the string periodically because the rushes shrink when they dry and may fall out of the bundle.

3. Soak the bundles for 1 hour in cold or warm water before you need to use them. Wrap them in a damp towel.

4. You can use rush whole as core material. You can also slit each rush lengthwise down one side with your thumbnail, open it up, again use your thumbnail to remove the pithy center, and use the remaining skin of the rush for stitching material. Keep rushes soaking or wrapped in a damp towel while you are working your basket. Use a knitting needle to open up a space between coils so you can slip the rush through in stitching (a yarn needle would break up the end of the rush).

Iris and Day Lily Leaves. Plants in the Iris family have long swordlike leaves set edge to edge and short-lived, showy flowers. The long leaves contain tough fibers that make them suitable for core and stitching material. The varieties of iris with leaves that are long and of narrow, uniform width are most desirable for basketmaking. One such variety of iris is blueflag *(I. versicolor)*, which is found in most of the eastern portion of North America in pond regions, marshes, and meadows. Cultivated iris of the beardless varieties include siberian iris *(I. siberica)* and yellow flag *(I. pseudacorus)*, also provide good leaves for basketmaking.

Day lilies have swordlike leaves that grow in dense clusters from the ground. The leafless flowering stem forks and forks again, each branch bearing a succession of flowers. The tawny day lily *(Hemerocallis fulva)*, a native of Eurasia, has escaped from American flower gardens and can commonly be found in thick masses along roadsides and in the borders of fields and woods. The long leaves have a fold that can be left folded or spread out flat when you use them in stitching coiled baskets.

Here are step-by-step instructions for preparing iris and day lily leaves for weaving:

1. Cut the leaves at the base of the plant no earlier than the first frost in the fall. The yellows, oranges, and rusts of the leaf color will indicate that it is time to cut. If the leaves are cut and dried while still green they will be brittle and less interesting in color.

2. Spread the leaves to dry on newspaper or stand them upright and loose in a large paper bag. Avoid bending the leaves or they may break.

3. Store the leaves in a cool, dry place.

4. Soak the leaves in cold to lukewarm water for 45 minutes to an hour before you want to use them. Soak only as many leaves at one time as you think you will need. Too much soaking, drying, and resoaking weakens the fiber and hastens decay.

5. Use the stiff or lower end of the leaf as its own needle when you stitch. You will need a bone awl or knitting needle to open a space or hole between the coils through which to slip the leaf end.

Inner Bark of Basswood. The inner bark of basswood *(Tilia americana)* was a favorite material of Indians for making cordage. It can be used in strips or twisted into 2-ply cord and used in coiled baskets. The cord makes a good stitching material and the strips may be used for both stitching and imbrication.

The following instructions will show you how to prepare strips of the inner bark of basswood:

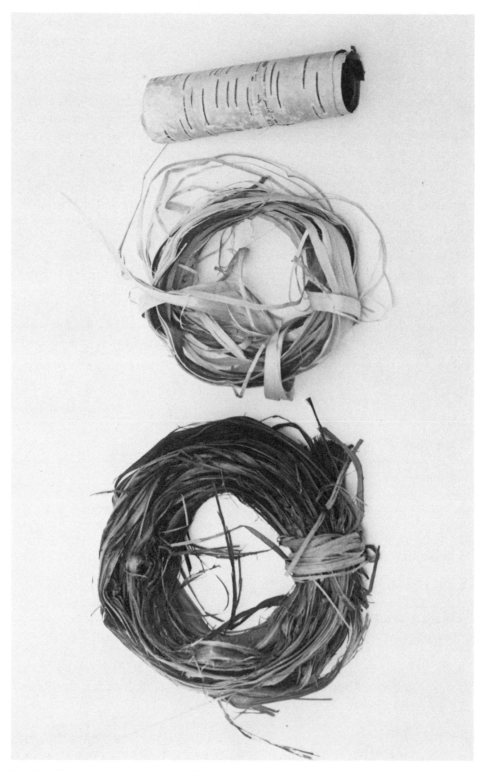

Barks. *These are some native barks that can be used in coiled basketry.*

1. Find a young basswood tree or sapling with a good length of trunk that is free of branches.

2. Cut the tree near the base and below the first branches.

3. Put the trunk in water and soak for 7 to 14 days. Slip the bark off the trunk as described under splint basketry, then soak the strips.

4. Separate the soft inner bark from the outer bark. It should just peel away from the spongy outer bark with no difficulty if the bark has been soaked long enough.

5. Coil the inner bark in loose loops and hang them to dry in a cool, dry place.

6. Cut the bark into strips for stitching and imbrication. Soak the strips in lukewarm water for 10 minutes before you use them. You can use a yarn needle when you stitch with this material.

Birch Bark. Paper birch *(Betula papyrifera)*, also called canoe birch, white birch, and silver birch, is the type of tree used by the Indians to make canoes. The bark was also used to make dishes, trays, and buckets or "macuks." Birch is commonly found in the open woods and along river banks throughout northern North America. This particular type of birch is especially suitable for baskets because the bark peels readily into long strips. The outer bark is a creamy white. The inner bark is a burnt orange. Birch bark strips can be used for stitching material and for imbricating coiled baskets.

Here are step-by-step directions for preparing birch bark:

1. Conserve trees by calling a local tree removal company and asking them to call you when a paper birch is coming down. They will often let you use the tree. The bark is most easily removed from the tree in June and July. An alternative would be to find a tree that is dying or dead and standing. The bark remains in good condition long after the tree dies.

2. Make a vertical cut 20″ to 25″ long in the tree trunk. Turn the bark back with one hand, passing it under the tree, and remove it with the other hand. The bark on the upper branches of the tree is often clearer and smoother than on the lower trunk.

3. If you are not going to use the bark right away, stack the strips between two wooden frames or boards. Tie the boards together or weight them down to prevent the sheets from curling up as they dry.

4. Cut the fresh bark into strips the desired width for your basket. The most common widths would be from ¼″ to ⅜″. You can also split the bark layers to the desired thickness.

5. If the bark has been dried in sheets, soften them by holding them over a fire. Move each sheet so it heats evenly. The bark should become as pliable as soft leather. Be careful not to hold it too close to the flame—remember that birch is an excellent tinder, is very flammable, and may scorch if you are not careful. When the bark is softened, prepare it as in Step 4.

6. When you stitch the basket, use a bone awl or knitting needle to open a hole between the coils and slip the bark strip through the opening. You may want to use a needle if the bark strips are very narrow.

Wild Grape Vine Bark. Wild grapes *(Vitis)* are usually high-climbing vines with shredding bark, alternate simple leaves, and forked tendrils. The fruits are round, pulpy berries that ripen in late summer or fall. They are important food for wildlife. While most wild grapes are too tart to be eaten raw, they make good preserves. The long, shaggy pieces of bark can be collected without harming the plant because the vine seems to be shedding them anyway. You can bunch these bark strips and use them dry as core material.

DYES

Raffia can be dyed very successfully with many natural dye materials. The subtle hues of vegetable dyes complement the quality of the raffia. You can get a variety of colors from a single dye bath by premordanting the raffia. When dyeing and premordanting, be sure to work in a well-ventilated area, use rubber gloves to protect your hands, and keep the mordant chemicals out of the reach of children. Several recipes for premordants as well as additional dyes are included here. Dyes listed in other Chapters may also be used to dye raffia.

You will need the following equipment for premordanting and dyeing.

Large Enamel Pans.

Wooden Spoons. Label a separate spoon for each premondant and for each dye.

Enamel Strainer.

Cheesecloth. Put the cheesecloth in the strainer and pour the contents of the dyebath through both.

Ivory Liquid. This is for washing the raffia.

Calgon. Use this if you have hard water.

Rubber gloves.

Scale. The scale should measure in ounces and pounds.

Clothesline or Newspaper. For drying raffia.

Measuring Spoons and Cup or Gallon Container.

Alum and Cream of Tartar. See the description under *Splint Basketry* and the instructions later in this chapter for dyeing and premordanting.

Chrome (potassium dichromate). This is a bright orange crystalline substance that, in solution, is very sensitive to light. Chrome is a poison, so avoid inhaling the fumes. Chrome will yield gold, brass, and rust colors.

Blue Vitriol (copper sulfate). This is a bright blue substance that can be bought as crystals or powder. The powder is preferable for dyeing because it dissolves more readily than the crystals. One of the main functions of copper sulfate as a mordant is to change yellow or yellow-green to a true green.

Hemlock Root Bark. Eastern hemlock *(Tsuga canadensis)*, also called Canadian hemlock, hemlock spruce, and spruce or hemlock pine, can be found throughout most of the eastern half of the United States. The needles are borne seemingly in one plane. The cones are small. The bark is thin, cinnamon red to purplish in color, and divided by narrow fissures into long, rough plates. In southern Appalachia the bark is used for dyeing wool a brown color. Hemlock dyes leather a red tone and is used in large quantities for tanning. For basketry you should use the bark from the roots. Look for hemlock roots where trees are being cleared from an area, especially along the banks of roads, streams, and rivers.

Scrape off the root bark with your jackknife (the roots themselves can be split and used for stitching material). For a half pound of raffia, put 8 ounces to 1 pound of root bark scrapings in an enamel pan. Remember that the amount of dyestuff determines the strength of the color. Cover the bark with 2 quarts to a gallon of soft water. Soak the bark for 3 days, then bring the dyebath to just under a simmer and maintain the heat for 3 to 6 hours. Add more water as it evaporates or cover the pan. Let the dyebath cool and then strain it through cheesecloth. You can try resoaking the bark overnight in another, smaller amount of water to see if the bark will yield any further dye.

Hemlock root bark dyes raffia pink without a premordant, pink-tan with alum, rust with chrome, and brown with copper sulfate.

Sassafras Bark. Sassafras *(Sassafras albidum)*, also known as saxifraxtree, sassafrac, or aguetree, ranges from southern Maine west to eastern Kansas and Oklahoma, and south to northern Florida and parts of Texas. Northern sassafras tends to be a small tree, commonly 20 feet tall. Farther south it may reach from 50 to 80 feet tall. The leaves, bark, twigs, and root of sassafrass are aromatic and often used in soaps, teas, and tonics. Young trees and new branches have large leaves with a characteristic 2-lobe mitten shape or 3-lobe shape where the center lobe is a little longer than the side lobes. Older branches have leaves with a simple boat shape. The bark is thin, reddish brown, and divided by shallow furrows when young. When the bark is old it is covered by thick scales and broad ridges separated by shallow furrows. To avoid damaging live trees you should strip bark from trees that have already been cut for clearing. The bark of older trees seems to yield a stronger dye.

Break the bark into small pieces. For a half pound of raffia put 8 ounces to a pound of bark into an enamel pan and cover with 1 gallon of soft water. Soak the bark for 2 or 3 days, then simmer for 2 to 5 hours or more. Add water as needed or cover the pan. The more concentrated the dyestuff, the darker the color you will get. Let the solution cool and then strain it through cheesecloth. Resoak the bark in another, smaller amount of water to see if the bark will yield any remaining dye.

Sassafras bark dyes raffia a light orange-tan with no premordant, orange-rust with alum, dark rust with chrome, and brown with copper sulfate.

Alder Bark. The alder shrub *(Alnus)* is commonly found throughout the northeastern and southern states. It is a large shrub that often forms thickets up to 15 feet high in damp, moist areas, beside streams, and in swamps. These

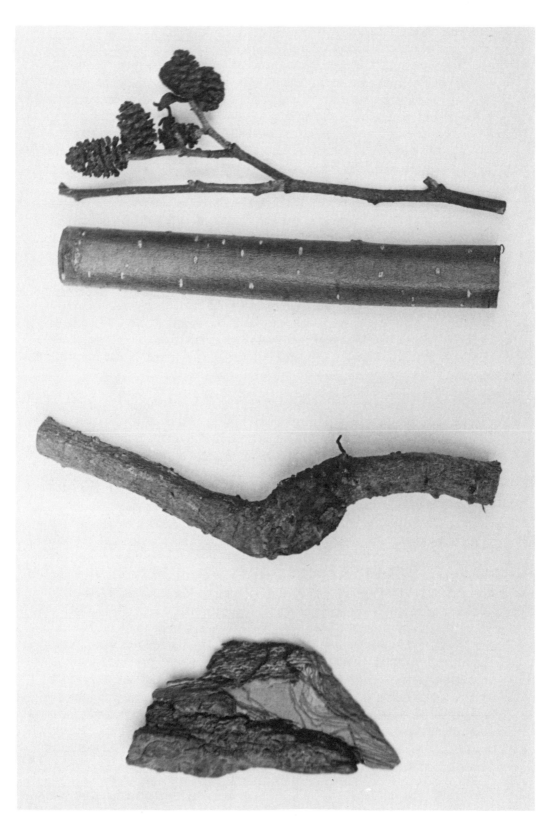

Dyestuffs. *You can use sassafras bark, hemlock root, and alder bark, for making dyes.*

thickets protect banks from excessive erosion and provide protection for small game birds. This alder may have a single smooth trunk, but it more frequently has a group of several stout stems. It is generally distinguished by clusters of small, woody, conelike fruits that persist through the second growing season, and by the elongated 3″ to 4″ catkins that are conspicuously present in winter. The bark is a smooth, gray-brown with pale gray horizontal markings or lenticels. Gather the stems and branches in winter or early spring.

Shave the bark off the alder stems and branches with your jackknife. For a half pound of raffia put 8 ounces to 1 pound of shavings in an enamel pan and cover with 1 gallon of soft water. Let the bark soak for 2 or 3 days and then bring the bath to a simmer. Simmer over low heat for 3 to 6 hours. Add more water as needed or keep the pan covered. Let the solution cool and strain it through cheesecloth.

Alder bark dyes raffia tan or light brown with no premordant, light green with alum, olive green with chrome, and pine green with copper sulfate.

PREMORDANTING AND DYEING

Here is how to prepare raffia for premordanting. Instructions for dyeing the premordanted raffia follow.

1. Loop the strands of raffia in a loose bundle.

2. Put the raffia in warm, soapy, soft water. Wash the raffia by squeezing it gently for about 3 minutes.

3. Rinse the raffia thoroughly.

4. Soak for 5 to 10 minutes in warm water until the raffia is completely transparent.

5. Add the raffia to the warm dye or premordant bath.

Alum Premordant

4 ounces raffia
1 gallon soft water
4 teaspoons alum (loose)
2 teaspoons cream of tartar (loose)

Measure the alum and cream of tartar without packing them too firmly in the spoon. It is better to have too little than too much. Dissolve the alum and cream of tartar in 1 cup of warm water and add this to the gallon of water, stirring to distribute the mordants evenly. Place the wet raffia in the mordant bath and bring the bath to a simmer over a low to medium heat. This should take about an hour. You can move the raffia around gently, but do not stir it too much. Reduce the heat and keep the bath just below simmering for another 45 minutes. Allow the raffia to cool in the bath, then rinse thoroughly in cold water. Dry the raffia by hanging it loosely on a clothesline or by spreading it out on newspaper. Store the dyed raffia in a paper bag in a closet for future use.

Chrome Premordant

4 ounces raffia
1 gallon soft water
¼ teaspoon chrome

Dissolve ¼ teaspoon chrome in 1 cup warm water and add this to the gallon of water, stirring to assure even distribution. Place the wet raffia in the mordant bath, cover it, and bring the bath slowly to a simmer over a low to medium heat (about 45 minutes to an hour). It is essential that the cover be kept on during mordanting for proper results. Move the raffia around several times in the bath, but be sure to replace the cover on the pan. When the bath reaches the simmering point, reduce the heat to just below simmering for another 45 minutes. The raffia can be left in the bath to cool. Rinse the raffia in cold water and either dye it immediately or wrap it in a towel or plastic bag and store it in a cool place such as the refrigerator. The raffia should not be exposed to light before dyeing or the color will be uneven. Properly stored, chrome-mordanted raffia may be kept for 3 or 4 weeks before using.

Copper Sulfate Premordant

4 ounces raffia
2 teaspoons copper sulfate
1 gallon soft water

Dissolve 2 teaspoons of copper sulfate in 1 cup of warm water and add this to the gallon of water, stirring to assure even distribution. Place the wet raffia in the mordant bath and bring the bath to a simmer over a low to medium heat (about 45 minutes to an hour). Move the raffia around in the bath several times. Reduce the heat and keep just below simmering for another 45 minutes. Let the raffia cool in the solution, then rinse in cold water. Dye the raffia immediately or dry it on a clothesline in the shade or spread it out on newspaper. Store the raffia in paper bags in a closet until you need to use it.

Raffia can be dyed with or without using a premordant.

1. Add the wet raffia to the dyebath.

2. Bring it slowly to a simmer (a half hour to 45 minutes). Lower heat and keep the dye just below simmering for 15 to 45 minutes.

3. Remove the dye from the heat and leave the raffia in the dyebath overnight.

4. Rinse the raffia in cold water until the water runs clear.

5. Hang the raffia to dry on a clothesline in a shady place.

GLOSSARY

Here are the terms you should know before you begin making coiled baskets:

Base. The initial surface area sewn in a spiral from the center.

Core. The foundation material used in a coiled basket. It should have strength and flexibility, and it should be larger than the stitching material in a given basket. It may be made of 1, 2, 3, 4, or 5 rods or a bundle of finer material such as grass.

Initial End. This is the end of an oval basket where you begin to bring up the side. Each new round of color or stitching should begin here.

Initial Stitch. The binding stitch in the beginning of a circular coiled basket that marks the beginning point for each new round.

Split Core. This is a core that is made up of more than 1 strand and is divided and stitched around separately at some point in the weaving.

Stitching Materials. Those strands that wrap around the core and stitch or bind the successive rounds of core together.

STITCHES

Here is a description of the most commonly used stitches in coiled basketry:

Lazy Squaw Stitch. This is technically a sewing pattern of wrap 1, stitch 1. The stitch encompasses two cores and holds them together. This pattern can be varied to include wrap 2, stitch 1; wrap 3, stitch 1; wrap 4, stitch 1, and so on. The stitches may be doubled (two lazy squaws side-by-side), tripled, or quadrupled to add strength to the binding or to vary the textural pattern in the surface design. The stitch is always placed between the stitches below, and finished stitches radiate from the center of the basket like spokes of a wheel.

Peruvian Stitch. This stitch is the same as the lazy squaw except that the stitches are placed either to the right or the left of the binding stitch below. The eventual stitch pattern forms a spiral emanating from the center of the basket. As the base and sides of the basket grow outward, new binding stitches are added and they begin a new series of rays.

Mariposa Stitch. Any of the lazy squaw variations but with the addition of a knot made around each stitch.

Split Mariposa Stitch. This is a double lazy squaw stitch where each of the stitches straddles the stitch below and then is knotted as in the mariposa.

Samoan Stitch. A lazy squaw stitch that is elongated by lifting up the core and then wrapping two or three times around the stitch as in the mariposa. This stitch opens up the framework of the basket and gives a perforated look to the surface.

Figure-eight Stitch. In this stitch the stitching crosses between the cores in the figure-eight rather than wrapping around. It is a hidden stitch in that it does not affect the surface texture of the basket. All you see are the rounds of coil.

Apache or Hook Stitch. This stitch hooks into the stitch below rather than wrapping around the two cores. There is no wrapping between stitches, so the core is left exposed. This is a particularly good stitch to use with baskets made of native materials.

Imbrication. A flat ribbon of decoration folded under and wrapped over the stitching to create a surface of rectangular blocks.

Oval Open-stitched Basket. *This basket by Cathy McNealy uses broombeard grass for the core and is wrapped with homespun linen stitching material. Pheasant feathers add further decoration.*

Coiled Baskets. *These patterned baskets by Sally Edmundson are, from left to right, raffia with reed core; cotton, wool, and rayon with seine twine core; and wool with cotton twine core.*

Serpent Basket. *Rope core, wool and chenille yarns, and metallic thread make up this innovative basket by Dolly Curtis that is embellished with Indian bells.*

Project Five

Oval-Based Coil Basket

This basket will give you experience with a variety of stitches and basic structural problems. It is also an exercise in using raffia. The raffia will be twisted as you work to give the appearance of sedge root. This is a time-consuming process, and after the first few rounds you may prefer not to twist the raffia, or to use another material such as linen, cord, or yarn.

Making coiled baskets is slow work, so don't be discouraged if you don't finish the basket in one sitting. Work on it a little at a time and let each new technique you learn suggest ideas for later basket shapes and surface designs.

MATERIALS

6 size 2 round reeds.

Raffia (1 or 2 ounces of good strands loosely looped).

¼″ ribbon about 15″ long, or a soft rush spike split.

A dozen or so small beads.

Scissors and thimble.

Garden snips.

Yarn needle and small blunt darning needle.

Nylon or heavy-duty thread.

4 small feathers.

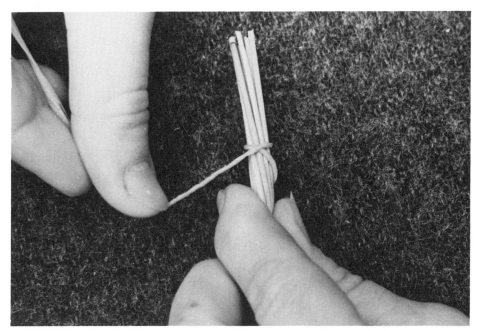

1. Hold the end of a length of raffia together with the ends of the 6 reeds. Hold both ends together in your left hand and twist the length of raffia between your thumb and forefinger, rolling it from right to left. Wrap the twisted raffia tightly around the reed core, crossing it as shown. Continue to wrap down the lengths of reed for 1½". Cut the beginning reed ends with garden snips.

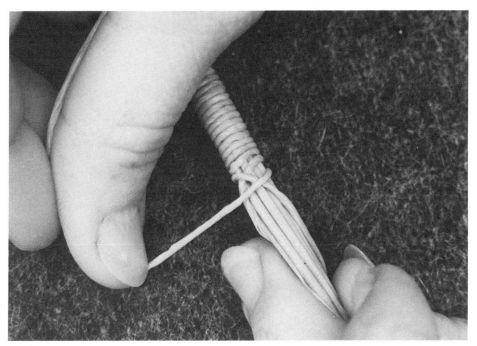

2. Add a new strand of raffia even though you may not have run out of your first strand yet (this is a good place to practice). Hold both ends of raffia against the core and wrap with the new end, keeping the cross on the right of the wrap. Continue wrapping until you have completed 2½".

3. *Wrap about 8 times more, making a bend in the core as you wrap. As soon as you have completed the turn wrap the raffia around both cores (a lazy squaw stitch). Wrap 4 more times around the single core, then over both cores again. Continue in this manner for the length of the base. Note that you are seeing the outside of the basket and working counter-clockwise.*

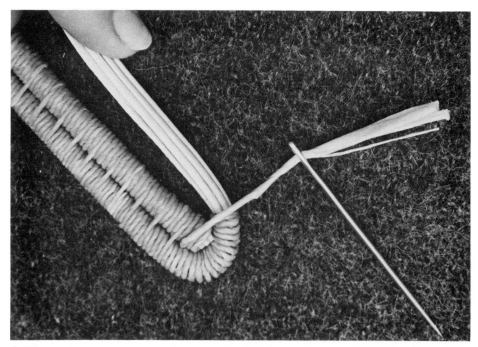

4. *Wrap around the turn at the other end of the base as shown. Then thread the raffia through a needle and make a lazy squaw stitch from your last wrap to the beginning end right after the turn. Keep wrapping down the length of the reed, making a lazy squaw stitch between those already made.*

5. *Keep each lazy squaw stitch centered between the stitches below. The number of wraps you will need between stitches will depend upon the varying thicknesses of raffia used. Keep in mind that the placement of the stitch is the important thing. Turn the next corner by making 4 lazy squaw stitches in the corner hole. This is the initial end of the basket. Each round of stitching will begin and end here. Now make two complete rounds of double lazy squaw stitches (wrapping twice around the 2 cores as shown).*

6. *Begin the side of the basket by pushing the core up on top of the last round of the base. The binding stitches (the lazy squaws) will appear longer on the outside and shorter on the inside. This round will use the Peruvian stitch. Do a double lazy squaw stitch, but place it on the left side of the stitch below.*

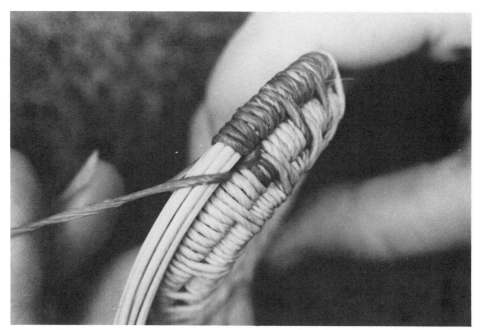

7. *Make the next round using the mariposa stitch. Make a double lazy squaw, placing it directly to the left of the stitch below as in the Peruvian pattern. Bring the raffia between the two cores, and wrap around the middle of the lazy squaw stitch from left to right as shown. Notice the pattern created by placing the stitches Peruvian style. Remember to bring up the sides of the basket and to work from the outside.*

8. *Make a complete round of split mariposa by splitting the double lazy squaw around the stitch below as shown. This will give you a vertical pattern of stitching.*

9. *Eventually you will need to replace the core reeds. The ends of the reed should be staggered so they do not all end in the same place. Taper the end of the new strand and insert it into the center of the core as far as you can.*

10. *Make a Samoan stitch by lifting the core away from the round below, making a lazy squaw stitch, and wrapping around the middle several times. The larger knot holds the core away from the round below and gives the basket an open look. Continue the next round in the Samoan stitch.*

11. Make a round using the figure-eight stitch as your binding stitch. Make several wraps, then bring the raffia around both cores in a figure-eight pattern as shown.

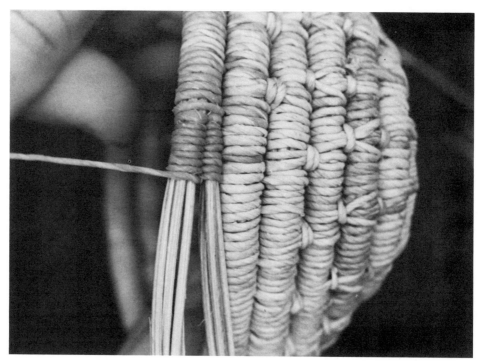

12. Split the core in half, and weave 5 figure-eight stitches around the 2 halves. On the 6th figure-eight, wrap around the core below as well to make an extended figure-eight. Complete the round in this manner. Then begin wrapping over the whole core in the figure-eight stitch for the next round.

13. *Continue using the figure-eight stitch for this round. Place your length of ribbon or rush as shown with the underside up, and wrap around the rush and core twice.*

14. *Fold the rush over along the core and wrap once around it to complete the imbrication. Reverse the rush again and wrap 2 times, then make the wrap around the front side again. Repeat the process once more, completing 3 simple imbrications. Next wrap around both the rush and the core 5 times.*

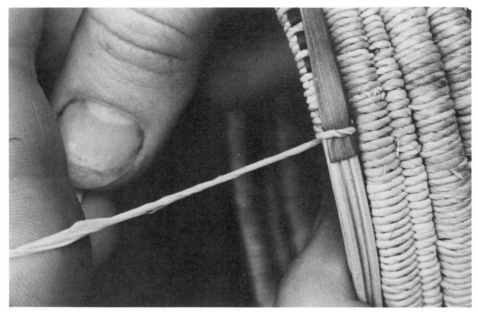

15. *For a more advanced imbrication, fold the ribbon against the core and wrap over the folded end 3 times.*

16. *Bring the rush over the wraps and repeat Step 15. Make 3 imbrications and wrap the core 5 times. Complete this round, alternating one set of imbrications with the other.*

17. *Continue using the figure-eight stitch for the next round. Place a feather over the core as shown and wrap several times over the shaft or vein of the feather to secure it. If the lower end of the feather is fluffy, you might want to pull the fluff off the shaft. Place your binding stitches on either side of the sections of imbrication below. An alternative to using the figure-eight stitch—for example if you don't want to stitch over your imbrication—is to make a hook (Apache) stitch as shown.*

18. *You can easily add beads to your basket. Thread a bead, then wrap the end of the thread along the core for a distance. Place the bead in position and continue wrapping. The wraps on either side of the bead should fit tightly together. The more thread wrapped before the bead is placed, the more secure the bead will be. You can add as many beads as you like, but stop as you begin the turn at the other end of the basket. Then add a feather by wrapping over the shaft or lower end as before.*

19. *Bend the feather back and wrap under the shaft. Wrap and stitch for about 1". Now add another feather in the same way. The two feathers should be pointing toward each other. Finish the round with more beads and a 4th feather pointing toward the first feather.*

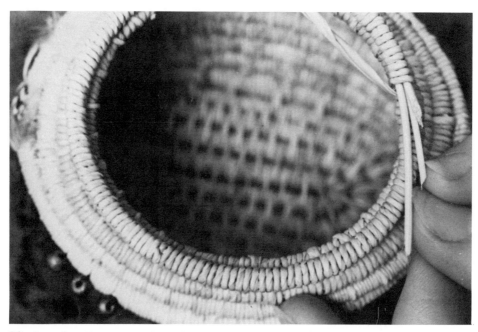

20. *Complete 5 more rounds in the figure-eight stitch or any stitch you like. Direct each round inward as you work to make the opening at the top of the basket smaller. Drop 1 reed in the core as you begin each of the last 3 rows. Try to make the last 2 rounds flair out slightly to finish off the shape. Cut the 3 remaining reeds as shown when you reach the end of the last round.*

21. *Finish the basket by wrapping the 3 tapered reed ends against the round below. Wrap over both cores as shown about 15 times. Use a small, blunt darning needle and thimble and stitch back under the last 5 wraps. Pull the raffia through and clip the remaining tail as close as possible.*

22. *Here is the finished basket. It serves as a sampler of the various stitches and decorative treatments possible in coiled basketry.*

Project Six

Round-Based Coil Basket

This basket will give you experience working with manmade materials and with colors. You will use a single rod core and will make a circular beginning and base. The Apache or hook stitch, used often in baskets made with native materials, is also introduced here.

A simple way to add color to a basket is to make one round with one color, then another round in a different color. The binding stitches will give some vertical direction to the design, but the predominate direction of the color is horizontal.

Vertical designs are created by consciously thinking through a pattern and adding the amount of color in each round that will contribute to the finished design. The number of designs possible in coiled basketry — geometric or organic, abstract or realistic—are endless.

You may prefer to use yarn, linen, or some other stitching material instead of the nylon cord suggested for this project.

MATERIALS

13 yards No. 7 braided polypropylene utility cord.

2 100 foot packages of No. 1 braided nylon mason line in a light color.

1¼ pound spool of size 18 twisted nylon twine in a dark color.

Scissors.

Large yarn needle and small blunt metal darning needle.

Matches (used to melt the ends of nylon rope to prevent unraveling).

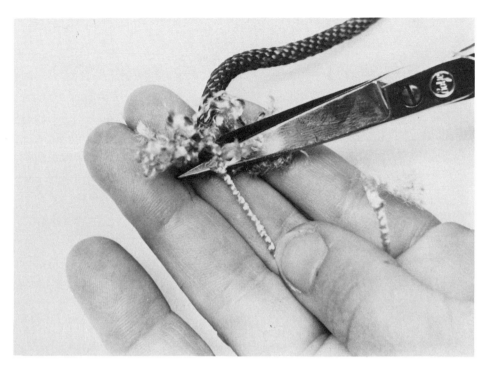

1. *Unravel the end of the polypropylene cord for about 1" and pull the inner core out about 3". Clip it off. This makes the beginning diameter of the core smaller and therefore tapered.*

2. *Cut a nylon stitching strand about 5 feet long. Place the short end along the core. With the long end in your right hand, wrap around the core and cross the strand as shown.*

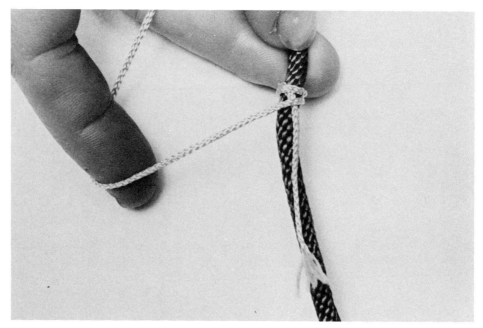

3. *Continue wrapping toward the short end of the stitching strand for about 1".*

4. *Bend the wrapped portion into a horseshoe shape as soon as you can, and making the smallest hole possible, wrap tightly over both cores. Clip the unraveled end of the core at an angle after the third wrap.*

5. *Complete 8 wraps, then thread the end of the stitching cord through the yarn needle. Make a figure-eight stitch as shown. Pull the stitch tight and wrap the core 2 times before making another figure-eight stitch. You can continue wrapping twice, stitching once all the way around the loop, or you can wrap 3 or 4 times between stitches to make faster progress.*

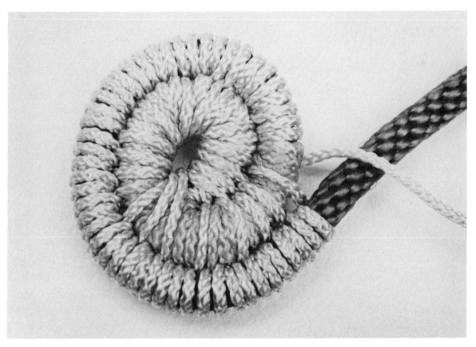

6. *Begin your second round when you reach the last of the 3 long stitches that go in the center hole. This is the initial stitch, and each new round of stitching will begin here. Stitch around the first round and the new core as shown. Do not stitch into the center hole beyond the first round.*

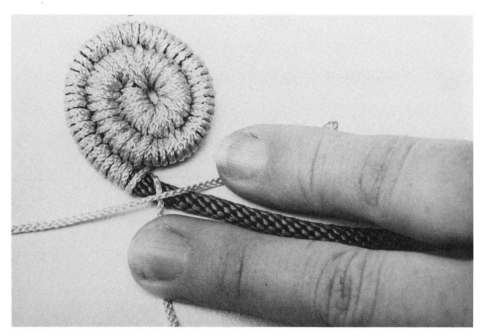

7. *Add a new stitching strand by crossing it with the end of the old one as shown. Hold these 2 ends along the core. Wrap the long end of the new strand around the core, keeping the crossing point to the left of your next wrap. Continue wrapping and stitching as before, concealing the two ends as you go along.*

8. *When you have completed 2 rounds of figure-eight stitching, begin spacing the wraps so the core is left exposed. Wrap 1, then stitch over both cores in a lazy squaw. Wrap 1 and stitch another lazy squaw. Continue around in this manner for one full round.*

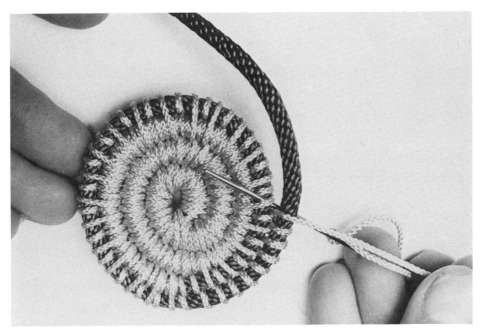

9. *Begin your second round of open stitching, but hook into the wraps and stitches below as shown. This is the Apache stitch. Notice that each wrap is a binding stitch. (Add new stitching strands by laying the ends under the open stitching on top of the core so they will be less obvious.) If you were to make a whole basket in the Apache stitch, you would eventually have to add wraps as the stitches would grow farther apart.*

10. *Complete 2 rounds using the Apache stitch. On the next round, wrap between the stitches as shown so the core is completely covered.*

11. For the next round you will need your dark color nylon. Add the new strand as shown, wrapping over the end with the light-colored strand to secure it along the core. When you begin the next round, twist the dark and light stitching strands so you will be stitching with the dark and wrapping it over the light. Later, clip the tail of the new strand close to the wrapping. Leave the light cord attached because you will pick it up again later.

12. Make this round using 3 wraps and 2 lazy squaw stitches. Remember to keep the lazy squaws centered between the stitches below. Remember, too, that the number of wraps between the stitches may vary. Begin the next round by twisting the strands again so you'll be working with the light strand. The light strand will be wrapped away from you, locking the dark strand along the core.

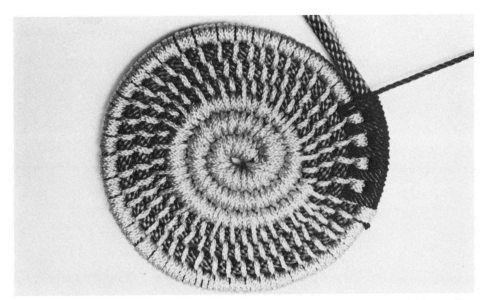

13. Stitch this round with the Peruvian stitch, placing the lazy squaws on the immediate left of the stitch below. Start the sides of the basket by pushing the coil up on the coil below. The base has been turned over here so you are looking at the basket from the inside and can clearly see the position of the core. Each round should be successively wider so the basket takes on a bowl shape. Turn the base back over and continue working the basket from the outside. Alternate rounds of dark and light in the Peruvian stitch until you have completed 8 rounds. The last round should be in a light color.

14. Begin making a vertical design on this next round by adding a new dark strand. Carry the strand along the core under the light wraps, except bring it out in a figure-eight stitch immediately to the left of each binding stitch below. Bring the sides of the basket in by placing each successive round on top of, but slightly to the inside of, the round below.

15. *In the next round, wrap the dark color twice around the core just above each dark stitch below. Add 3 more rounds, increasing the number of dark wraps with each round. You will begin to see long vertical triangles forming. Make the last 3 rounds of the basket in the solid dark color. As you work these rounds, place the coils one directly on top of the other.*

16. *Complete the last round except for the last 2" of core. Unravel the core, then pull out the inner core about 1" and clip it off. Wrap and stitch for another inch.*

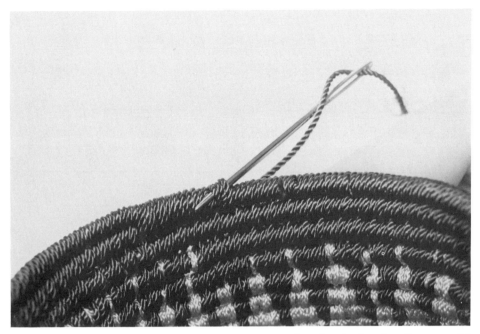

17. Wrap over both cores for the last inch. Stitch back under the last 3 to 5 wraps with a small darning needle and pull the end of the stitching cord through. Clip the end of the core as close to the wrapping as possible.

18. Here is your finished two-color basket. You can pre-plan such baskets, or you can let the designs grow as you work.

TWINED BASKET

This basket by Carol Hart uses reed, sisal, linen, and homespun wool. The different fibers give this simply-constructed basket a sense of texture and pattern as well as color.

Twined Basketry

The word twine has its origins in the Middle English word *twin*, meaning a rope of 2 strands. To twine is to twist together. You have already been introduced to the technique of twining since it is one of many weaves used in wicker work. A twined basket has a set of round or flat vertical spokes that are usually spaced more closely than in wicker basketry. Two or more horizontal weavers, also either round or flat, twist around each other as they weave around the spokes.

Some of the finest baskets made by the Indians were twined. The twisted weavers held the spokes firmly in place. Soft twined baskets used delicate warp elements, usually grasses or thin strands of bark or root fiber. Stiff twined baskets used stronger, heavier elements such as willow. Open twined utility baskets — such as pack baskets, seed beaters, and fish traps — were made by leaving space between rounds of twining to expose the spoke materials.

ROUND REEDS

Reeds make good spoke material for baskets twined with raffia or native materials as weavers. They can be used both as spokes and weavers in openwork twined baskets. Use the size of reed that is appropriate to the size basket you want to make. Sizes 1 and 2 are good to use for weavers, and larger sizes can be used for spokes. See *Wicker Basketry* for instructions on preparing round reeds.

RAFFIA

Raffia can be dyed in earth tones and twisted tightly to mimic roots. Both its ability to take dye and its flexibility make it a good material to use in weaving twined baskets. See *Coiled Basketry* for directions on preparing raffia.

RUSH, GRASS, AND FIBERS

Both rush and grass are sturdy materials that can be used for spokes. Soak the grass briefly. Straighten the pieces and let them dry before using to make the grass easier to control.

Jute, sisal, nylon, linen, and other cords that have strength and body can be successfully used as spoke and weaving material. Because these fibers are flexible, expect that the resulting baskets will also be flexible. If tightly twined, however, the basket form will have enough rigidity to hold its shape.

All sorts of yarns can be used for weavers. Try goat's hair, horsehair, or camel's hair yarn. Cotton, linen, wool, acrylic, rayon, and nylon are some others that work well. The color and texture of each type of yarn will contribute to the finished statement of the basket.

THE CARE OF TWINED BASKETS

Make sure your hands are clean while you are making baskets from fibers. As soon as baskets twined with yarns, jutes, linen, cotton, and like materials are finished, spray them thoroughly with a sealer such as Scotch Guard. This will make them easier to keep clean. Remember not to put baskets made of fibers in direct sunlight or they may fade.

Commercial Materials. *The materials available for twined basketry include homespun wool, Greek wool, reed, raffia, waxed linen, jute, sisal, Persian wool, metallic cord, and linen.*

Natural Materials. *Here are some native plant materials for twined basketry: corn husk, white pine bark, basswood cordage, and rye grass.*

TOOLS AND EQUIPMENT

You will need the following items for preparing native materials:

Plastic Dish Pan.

Knitting, Yarn, and Darning Needles.

Scissors and Pruning Shears.

Sharp Jackknife.

Pliers.

Measuring Tape.

Glycerin. Add 1 teaspoon per quart of warm soaking water to keep reed, raffia, and other materials from becoming brittle.

WILD AND GARDEN MATERIALS

Some of the native materials discussed in the previous chapters can also be used for twined baskets. Honeysuckle vines, split willow branches, and other shoots can be used for spokes. Cattail leaves can be used for both spoke and weaving materials. Wisteria runners can be split and used for spokes. The bark can be peeled off, dried, soaked, and then used for weavers. Rushes and strips of the inner bark of basswood can also be used for weavers.

Basswood Cordage. Basswood cordage can be used as weaving material in twined baskets. Prepare the basswood strips as described in Coiled Basketry. The demonstration shows how to prepare 2-ply cordage from basswood strips.

Inner Bark of White Pine. White pine *(Pinus strobus)* is a large, plumey foliaged evergreen tree that grows up to 100 feet high and 3 feet in diameter. It ranges throughout the eastern United States in areas having light sandy soil. It is northern New England's most important lumber tree—white pine timber formed the tall masts and spars of the New England clipper ships. The slender needles grow in clusters of 5 up to 5″ long, and fall at the end of the second season. The bark on young trees is smooth and on older trees it is dark and rough. The cones are 4″ to 6″ long, narrow, and slightly curved. White pine branches spring out in whorls around the trunk, and one new whorl is produced each year. Spring is a good time to gather the bark.

If you do not have a stand of white pine that needs thinning, call your local tree removal service and ask when one is coming down. Remove the bark as soon as possible after the tree is cut, preferably the same day. To minimize waste, score the bark in 3″ or 4″ strips before pulling it off. Dry and store the bark in paper sacks until you are ready to use it.

The following demonstration gives step-by-step directions for preparing pine bark for weaving.

Corn Husks. The husks of all types of corn can be used. Sweet corn husks are whiter and finer in texture, however Indian corn has larger, stronger husks. Prepare the husks by simply removing them from the corn and spreading them

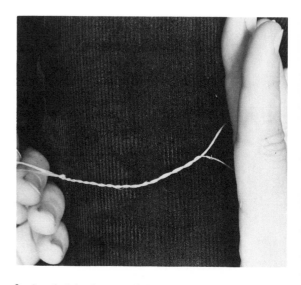

1. *Knot the ends of two 1/16" wide strips of basswood bark and hold the strips in your left hand.*

2. *Sandwich the parallel strips between your thigh and the fingers of your right hand. Roll the strips away from you, keeping them parallel. The more tightly the strands are twisted, the tighter the cordage twist will be. Hold the twisted strands under the palm of your hand.*

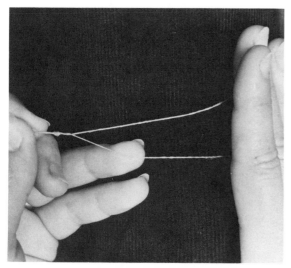

3. *Twist the knot in your left hand away from you. This twists the strands around each other and makes a 2-ply cord. Hold the cord at the point where the strands converge, then repeat the last two steps.*

4. *Add a new strand by overlapping the ends as shown and rolling them together as in Step 2. (If they do not mesh, try shredding the ends with a comb before rolling.) Splicing should be staggered so new pieces are not added all at one time. Trim the hairy ends after splicing.*

White Pine Bark

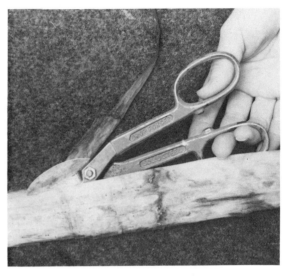

1. Soak the dried bark for 10 to 15 minutes until it is soft and pliable. Bend the bark to crack the corky outer bark, then pull the outer bark away from the inner bark.

2. Trim off the rough edges of the inner bark, then cut the bark into ½" strips. These strips will be thick, and there may be a layer of spongy outer bark covered with beads of pine gum (resin). Scrape the spongy layer off with your jackknife.

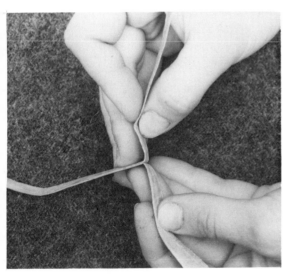

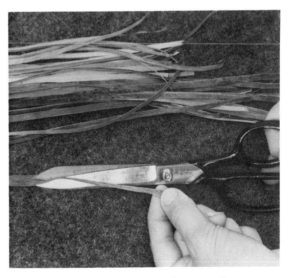

3. Split the remaining strip of inner bark as shown.

4. Cut these thin strips into ⅛" or 1/16" widths. The strips can be dried and stored in a paper bag. Soak the strips before using them, keep them wrapped in a damp towel while working, and keep your fingers wet while you weave.

separately on newspaper to dry. Another way to prepare them is to pull the husks back away from the corn cob and hang the whole thing in a cool, dry place. When you are ready to use them, soak them in warm water for a few minutes until soft. If the husks are brittle, add glycerin to the soaking water.

Husks become mildewed when stored in warm, humid conditions. Bleach mildew spots out of the husks by putting them in a solution of ¼ cup liquid laundry bleach to ½ gallon of water. Check the husks every 5 to 10 minutes to see if the spots are disappearing. It usually does not take more than a half hour. The less time the husks are in the bleach the better. Rinse the husks thoroughly in clean water.

Keep the husks in a damp towel as you use them. Split them into narrow strips with your fingernail or cut them with scissors to the required width.

Rye Grain Stalks. Buy rye grain seed from Agway or some other seed supplier in late August. Plant the seed in September. This rye grows about 4 feet tall and has a large tassel. It is usually harvested for grain the following July. You can harvest it for basketry about the same time. Dry the grass by spreading it out on newspaper. If you want it to retain some of its green color, dry it in the shade or indoors. If you want a yellow color, dry it in the sun so it will bleach. Prepare it for twining by cutting the stalks at the nodes. Cut the nodes off. Soak the stalks in water for about 20 minutes or until soft. Split the stalk with your fingernail into the desired widths for twining. Keep them rolled in a damp towel as you work. Rye grass can also be used in bundles for core material.

DYES

Raffia, corn husks, and other materials used for twining can be colored with dyes mentioned in previous chapters as well as with the dyes that follow.

Here are the tools and equipment you will need for dyeing:

Enamel Pans and Wooden Spoons.

Colander or Strainer.

Cheesecloth.

¾ Cup Rusty Nails. A rusty railroad spike or the equivalent could be used instead of nails.

Wooden spoons.

Alum.

Soft Water or Rainwater.

Red Maple Bark. Red maple *(Acer rubrum)*, also called swamp maple or water maple, is a medium size tree 40 to 50 feet high with a trunk diameter of 2 to 4 feet. It is common in swamps, in low wet woods, or on the borders of streams. It is found throughout New York and New England and ranges from southern Newfoundland to Minnesota, west to the Dakotas and south to Texas and Florida. The bark is a smooth, light brown-gray on young trees, but very dark and furrowed into long ridges on old trees. The buds, flowers, summer twigs,

Dyestuffs. *Here are pieces of red maple bark stripped from a sapling and a rusty iron spike used for the mordant.*

and autumn leaves are broadly 3-lobed, less often 5-lobed, with angles between the lobes and toothed leaves. The bark is easily removed from branches or saplings in the spring and early summer. Red maple saplings are abundant in wet thickets where thinning will benefit the remaining trees.

Here are the directions for preparing red maple bark dye for a half pound of raffia:

1. Strip the bark from the sapling as soon as it is cut. Cut the bark into small pieces.

2. Put ½ to 1 gallon of bark chips in an enamel pan. Cover the chips with soft water and let soak for as long as a week.

3. Bring the dyebath to a boil and simmer for 2 hours or more. Cover the pan or replenish the water as it evaporates.

4. Remove the bath from the heat and let it stand overnight or for several days. The longer it stands the darker the color will get.

5. Strain the dyebath through a colander and cheesecloth. Add the wet raffia to the bath and bring it to a simmer. Simmer 25 minutes, turning from time to time. Remove from heat and let stand overnight. The color without a mordant should be a pinkish tan. With alum the color is a golden brown, and with a rusty railroad spike the color is an olive brown.

Common St. John's Wort Leaves. Common St. John's wort (*Hypericum perforatum*) is the most familiar of the St. John's worts. It has black dots on the margins of the yellow flower petals and translucent dots on the leaves. It grows 1 to 2½ feet high and is found along roadsides and in fields throughout the United States from June through September.

Here are instructions for preparing St. John's wort dye for a half pound of raffia:

1. Crush 3 to 4 quarts of leaves and put them in an enamel pan.

2. Cover the leaves with soft water and bring this to a boil. Reduce the heat, cover the pan, and boil for 35 minutes.

3. Strain the bath and discard the leaves. Add enough cold soft water to make a half gallon of dye solution.

4. Dissolve 6 tablespoons of alum in cold water and add it to the bath. Stir until the alum is dissolved.

5. Add the wet raffia and simmer the dyebath for 25 minutes. Turn the raffia from time to time to ensure even dyeing. Remove the bath from the heat and let stand overnight. The color with alum should be green.

GLOSSARY

The following terms will be helpful in understanding the step-by-step directions in the following twined basket projects:

Cross Warp. The spokes cross each other and are twined into that position.

Common St. John's Wort. *This flower gives a green dye when used with an alum mordant.*

Lattice Twine or T-Twine. A stiff cross spoke is laid horizontally behind the vertical spokes. Two flexible weavers are wrapped around the resulting crosses.

Openwork Twining. Openwork is made with stiff spokes and flexible weavers in the plain or twill techniques. It is characterized by an open space between rounds of horizontal weave.

Plain Weave. Two weavers twist around each of the spokes. There is a vertical pattern to this weave.

Side Round. The rounds counted from the turn of the basket rather than from the beginning.

Three-Strand Twining. Three weavers are used instead of two, giving a longer winding rope appearance. It is strengthening as well as decorative and used especially at the bottom of baskets where there is more stress.

Turn of the Basket. The point where the base turns to become the sides.

Twill Weave. Two weavers, but each twist wraps two or more warps. The weave separates the pairs in each line of superimposed round. There is a diagonal pattern to this weave.

Catalpa Basket. This airy basket by Pat Malarcher combines split catalpa pods arranged in a woven fashion with waxed linen twining around the edges.

Twined Basket with Feathers. *A Hong Kong grass warp combines with a linen, jute, and sisal weft in this basket by Pat Malarcher that is further decorated with feathers.*

Project Seven

Round-Based Twined Basket

This basket has a simple round beginning. The shape of the basket is determined by controlling the existent groups of spokes rather than by adding or subtracting. Dividing the groups of spokes allows for different degrees of texture. Because there can always be an even number of spoke groups, a large variety of patterns and designs are possible. The weaves used in this project are plain twine, triple twine, and twill twine. The final look of this basket can be varied by your choice of materials for weavers and by your control of the shape.

MATERIALS

40 strands of Irish sisal (or jute), each cut 1 foot 3″ long.

4 or 5 sisal weavers each 5 or 6 feet long.

3 wool weavers in a light color, each 5 or 6 feet long.

2 or 3 marlin twine, cord, or wool weavers, each 5 or 6 feet long, in a dark color.

2 waxed linen weavers, each 5 or 6 feet long, in a dark and a light color.

Scissors.

Yarn needle and blunt darning needle.

1. Wrap several times around the center of the bundle of spokes with the center of a weaver as shown.

2. Count out 10 spokes at the edge of the bundle and twine the two weavers around them. This is your initial spoke. It is a good idea to attach a piece of colored yarn to the initial spoke to make it easier to see. Divide the rest of the bundle into groups of 10, and twist around each group with the pair of weavers.

3. Pull the spokes apart as you twine so they become like the spokes in a wheel.

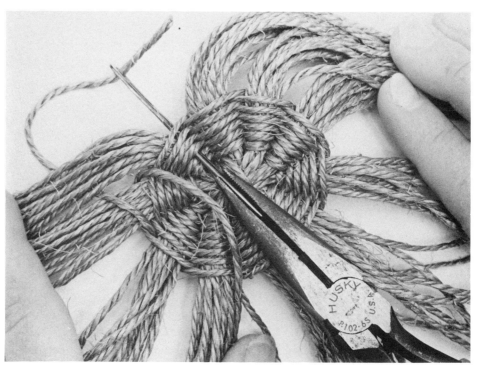

4. When a weaver runs out, thread the end through a yarn needle and pull it down into the weaving as shown.

5. *Pull the end of the new weaver through in the same manner and continue twining. Cut the ends off close to the weaving after making 1 or 2 rounds with the new weaver.*

6. *Complete 9 rounds, bringing the base toward you in a slight saucer shape. Separate the spokes now into groups of 5 strands each.*

7. *Turn the basket by bending the spokes down and away from you as you weave. On the 6th round of twining around the 5-strand spokes, drop one of the light weavers at the initial spoke and add a dark weaver. This will give you a vertical stripe pattern.*

8. *As you begin your 10th round, drop the light weaver and add 2 more dark weavers. Remember to add them at the initial spoke. Make a triple twine weave as shown, always twining with the weaver on your left. Make 2 rounds. Keep the shape of the basket sloping upward by holding the spokes in an upright position as you weave.*

9. End the 3 weavers at the initial spoke. Add another color by doubling the weaver as shown. Make 2 rounds in this new color.

10. Replace one of the weavers with one of wool or any yarn with a fluffier texture. Twine 2 or 3 rounds.

11. Separate the spokes into groups of 2 using the plain twine. Make 2 rounds.

12. Replace the yarn weavers with waxed linen weavers. Make 4 rounds of plain twine. Bring the shape of the basket in by pushing the spokes toward the center as you weave.

13. Make 2 more rounds using wool weavers, then make another round with waxed linen. As you begin the 2nd round of linen, twine around 1 spoke rather than 2 on the first stitch. Make the rest of the round twining around 2 spokes. This creates the stair-step pattern of the twill twine. Pull the spokes toward you as you weave to bring the basket shape out again.

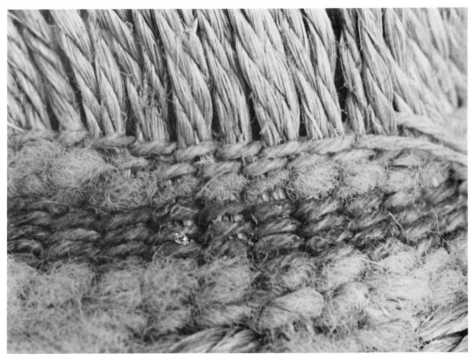

14. Maintain the twill twine by twining around 1 spoke at the beginning of each round.

15. *Add yarn weavers and weave 3 more rounds of plain twine. Then add waxed linen weavers.*

16. *Make 1 round of waxed linen, separating the spokes so you are twining around 1 spoke at a time. Then add a wool weaver for the final round. The thicker yarn twining around 1 spoke at a time helps to expand the shape. Stitch the end of yarn into the weaving below.*

17. Cut off the spoke ends as shown, making sure the fringe is even all around.

18. Your finished basket will look something like this. Variations can be made by changing the patterns, dividing the spokes in other arrangements, using a different variety of materials, making the basket larger, and experimenting with the shape. Feathers and beads can be added, and spokes can be taken out, wrapped separately, and twined back into the body of the basket.

Project Eight

Twined Openwork Basket

This project demonstrates a second type of beginning for a twined basket. Openwork, cross-warp twining, and the lattice weave are introduced. Plain and triple weaves are also used in this basket.

MATERIALS

10 size 3 round reed spokes, each cut 1 foot 6″ long.

63 or 64 size 3 round reed spokes, each cut 8″ long and tapered at one end.

12 to 14 size 1 round reed weavers.

Knitting needle.

Tin snips or heavy scissors.

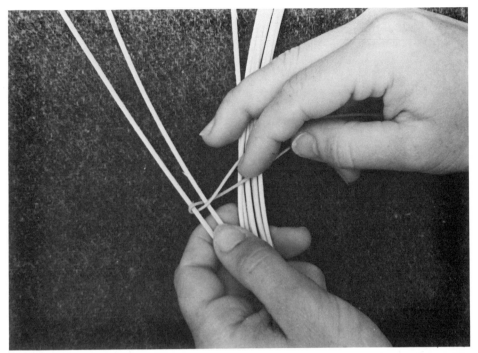

1. *Bend a weaver in half and twist it around the center of a long spoke as shown. The first spoke you twist around will become your initial spoke.*

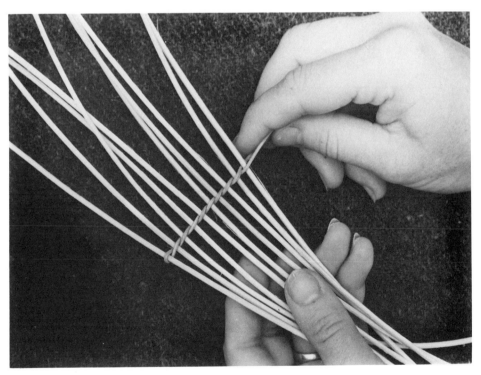

2. *Twine tightly around all 10 spokes.*

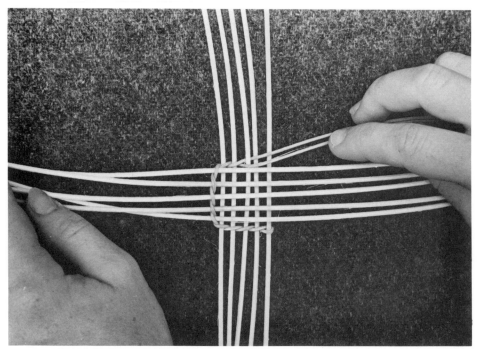

3. Cross half the spokes over the other half as shown, and continue twining. Leave about ¼″ to ½″ of space between rounds in openwork.

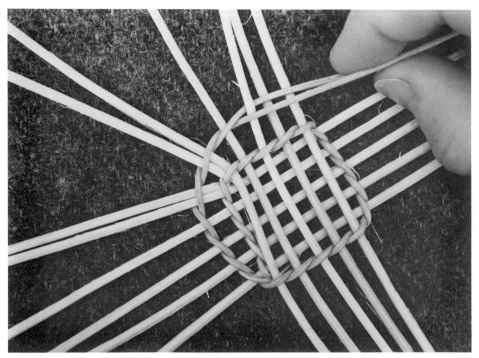

4. As you begin the second round, insert the tapered ends of 2 short spokes into the weave of each of the 4 corners.

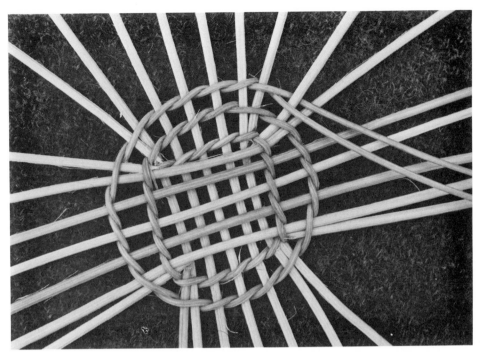

5. Twine these double corner spokes separately as you make the third round.

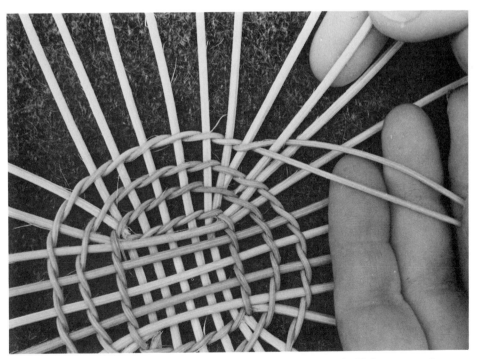

6. Add more spokes in the corner as you make your 4th round. If the new spokes are secured tightly you can twine them separately as you insert them. Add spokes from now on whenever and wherever you need them.

7. Close the space between rows as you make your 5th round and prepare to turn the basket. This gives the basket a firmer foundation and makes turning the basket easier.

8. When you run out of a weaver, insert a new weaver on the left of a spoke as shown.

9. *Tuck the end of the old weaver into the twining to the right of the spoke. Bring the new weaver behind the spoke and continue twining.*

10. *Add a third weaver as you begin your 7th round to begin the 3-strand twine. Carry the left-hand weaver over 2 spokes and behind the 3rd spoke each time.*

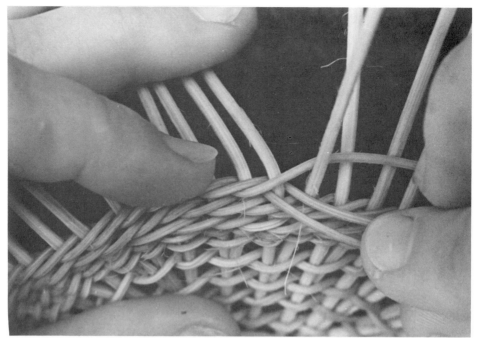

11. *Make 2 rounds of 3-strand twining before turning the basket. Bend the spokes away from you and make a final round of 3 strand twining. This should set the spokes in a vertical position. Make a round of plain weave before you begin the openwork again.*

12. *The basket will be cylindrical if you continue with the spokes in a vertical position and close together. To make the shape flair out, or to add interest to the pattern, add new spokes between every other spoke. Use a knitting needle to open up a space in the weave before inserting the new spoke. Shape the basket by applying pressure on the spokes as you weave.*

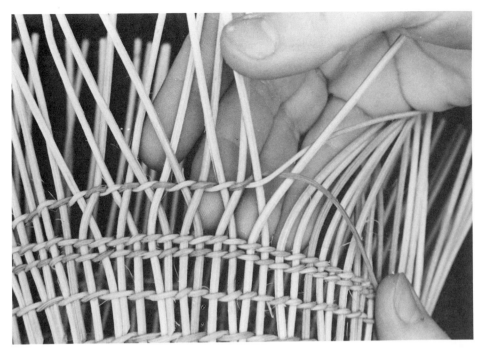

13. Add interest to the pattern of your openwork by spacing some rounds closer than others. As you begin the 9th round on the sides, twist each pair of spokes so they cross each other as shown and twine them into that position. This is called crossing the warp and cross-warp twining.

14. If you run out of weaver in cross warping, an alternative method of adding a new one is to hold the 2 ends together as shown. The new weaver is inserted into the twining from the front to the back. Continue twining. The ends will be twined against spokes in the next round.

15. *Make 3 more rounds of plain twine. Lay a size 3 reed cross spoke on the inside of the basket and twine over it. This is the lattice weave. If you find it awkward to weave through the spokes, trim the ends down so they stand about 1" above the weave. Then weave 1 or 2 more rounds. Make a final round of plain weave. Twine as tightly as you can.*

16. *Look carefully at the top several rounds of weave—this border may appear wavy or uneven. Use a knitting needle to adjust the top of the basket so the top round is as level as possible. Clip off the remaining spokes.*

17. *This basket is good for onions or fruit because they will be well ventilated. It also makes an attractive planter. Many variations are possible by combining the weaves in different ways or by using other materials for weavers. You might want to try closing the weave for sections of the basket. Use suggestions in the chapter on wicker basketry for rim ideas. You may need to thin the spokes at the rim of a twined basket before weaving a wicker-type border.*

Suppliers List

A.A.A. Cordage Co.
3238 N. Clark Street
Chicago, Illinois 60657
Twine, rope

AC/DC
Box 484
Cherokee, North Carolina
Beads, brown beadcorn

Ace Rattan Products
60-19 54th Place
Maspeth, New York 11378
Rattan

Artisan House Materials
80 Main Street
Northport, New York 11768
Beads, bells, cords

Bamboo and Rattan Works
901 Jefferson Street
Hoboken, New Jersey 07030
Bamboo, rattan

Dick Blick Art Materials
P.O. Box 1267
Galesburg, Illinois 60614
Basket materials, cords, yarns

Lee Bristol Nursery
Route 55
Sherman, Connecticut 06784
*Botanist: mail-order service
for iris and day lilies*

Cane and Basket Supply Co.
1283 S. Cochran Avenue
Los Angeles, California 90019
Fibers, reed, raffia, sea grass

CCM Arts and Crafts
9520 Baltimore Avenue
College Park, Maryland 20740
Cords, yarns, basketry supplies

The Clay People
3345 N. Halstead
Chicago, Illinois 60657
*Exotic beads: African, coconut
togo, snake, clam, brass*

Coulter Studios
118 East 59th Street
New York, New York 10022
Reed, sea grass, yarns

Creative Handweavers
P.O. Box 26480
Los Angeles, California 90026
*Cords, jute, palm strips, reed,
unusual yarns*

Earth Guild Inc.
149 Putnam Avenue
Cambridge, Massachusetts 02139
*Dyes, mordants, basket
materials, yarns*

Earthworks
264 West Willow
Chicago, Illinois 60614
Handcrafted Beads

Frederick J. Fawcett
129 South Street
Boston, Massachusetts 02111
Linen yarns

Freed Co.
Box 394
Albuquerque, New Mexico 87103
*Beads, coral, wampum strands,
leather, shells*

Gettinger Feather Corp.
38 West 38th Street
New York, New York 10008
Natural and dyed feathers

P.C. Herwig Co.
Route 2, Box 140
Milaca, Minnesota 56353
Linen, jute, sisal, rayon

Imported Findings
Please Complex
Main Street
Chester, Massachusetts 01011
Beads, feathers

Lemco
P.O. Box 40545
San Francisco, California 94140
Beads, fibers, yarns

Lily Mills Co.
Shelby
North Carolina 28150
Cords, jute, chenille, yarns

The Mannings—Creative Crafts
East Berlin
Pennsylvania 17316
*Cotton, linen, yarns, beads,
dyes, books*

Naturalcraft
2199 Bancroft Way
Berkeley, California 94704
*Beads, cords, feathers, yarns,
basket supplies*

The Niddy Noddy
416 Albany Post Road
Croton-on-Hudson, New York 10520
*Beads, dyes, fleece, basket supplies,
yarns, cords, books*

New Hampshire Cane and Reed Co.
65 Turnpike Street
Suncook, New Hampshire 03275
Reed, cane, splints, raffia

Northwest Handcraft House
110 West Esplinade
North Vancouver, British Columbia
Canada
Dyes, manila, raw sisal, yarns

H.H. Perkins Co.
Dept. S.P.
10 South Bradley Road
Woodbridge, Connecticut 06525
*Cane, fibers, reed, raffia, rush,
sea grass, splints, books*

Riverside Crafts
1654 N. Cleveland
Chicago, Illinois 60614
*Beads: Ceramic, copper, brass,
silverplate*

School Products Co.
1201 Broadway
New York, New York 18001
Cotton, homespun, linen, wool

Whitaker Reed Co.
90 May Street
Box 172
Worcester, Massachusetts 01602
Round and flat reed

Willow Craft
9 Willow Lane
Great Neck, New York 11023
Waxed Linen

World Wide Herbs
11 St. Catherine Street East
Montreal, Canada
Dyes

Bibliography

Basketry

Allen, Elsie. *Pomo Basketmaking*. Healdsburg, California: Naturegraph 1972.

Blanchard, Mary Miles. *The Basketry Book*. New York: Charles Scribner's Sons, 1916.

Butler, Eva L. and Hadlock, Wendel S. *Uses of Birchbark in the Northeast*. Rockland, Maine: Seth Low Press, 1957. (Robert Abbe Museum, Bulletin VII, Bar Harbor, Maine.)

Christopher, F.J. *Basketry*. New York: Dover, 1952

Eaton, Allen H. *Handcrafts of New England*. New York: Bonanza.

————*Handcrafts of the Southern Highlands*. New York: Dover 1973.

Facklam, Margery and Patricia Phibbs. *Corn Husk Crafts*. New York: Sterling Publishing Co., 1974.

Horowitz, Elinor Lander. *Mountain People, Mountain Crafts*. Philadelphia and New York: J.B. Lippincott Co., 1974.

James, George W. *Indian Basketry and How to Make Indian and Other Basketry*. Glorieta, New Mexico: Rio Grande Press, Inc., 1970.

Leftwich, Rodney L. *Arts and Crafts of the Cherokee*. Cullowhee, North Carolina: Land-of-the-Sky Press, 1970.

Lyford, Carrie A. *Ojibwa Crafts*. Washington D.C.: U.S. Dept. of Interior, 1943.

Mason, Otis T. *Aboriginal American Basketry*. U.S. National Museum Annual Report for 1902. Glorieta, New Mexico: Rio Grande Press, 1970.

Meilach, Dona. *A Modern Approach to Basketry*. New York: Dover, 1972.

Miles, Charles and Bovis, Pierre. *American Indian and Eskimo Basketry*. New York: Bonanza, 1969.

Navajo School of Indian Basketry. *Indian Basket Weaving*. New York: Dover, 1971.

Newman, Sandra C. *Indian Basket Weaving*. Flagstaff, Arizona: Northland Press, 1974.

Paul, Francis. *Spruce Root Basketry of the Alaska Tlingit*. U.S. Dept. of Interior, Bureau of Indian Afairs, 1944.

Robinson, A.E. *The Basket Weavers of Arizona*. Albuquerque: University of New Mexico Press, 1954.

Rossbach, Ed. *Basketry as Textile Art*. New York: Van Nostrand Reinhold, 1973.

Schneider, Richard C. *Crafts of the North American Indian*. New York: Van Nostrand Reinhold, 1972.

Speck, Frank G. *Decorative Art of the Indian Tribes of Connecticut*. Ottawa Geological Survey, Memoir 75, No. 10. Anthropological Series, 1915.

Speck, Frank G. and Butler, Eva L. *Eastern Algonkian Block-Stamp Decoration. Addendum: Some Early Indian Basketmakers of Southern New England.* Trenton, New Jersey: Archeological Society of New Jersey, 1947.

Tod, Osma Gallinger. *Earth Basketry.* New York: Bonanza, 1972.

Wheat, Margaret M. *Survival Arts of the Primitive Paiutes.* Reno, Nevada: University of Nevada Press, 1967.

Whiteford, Andrew Hunter. *North American Indian Arts.* New York: Golden Press, 1970.

Wigginton, Eliot (Ed.). *The Foxfire Book.* Garden City, New Jersey: Anchor Books, Doubleday, 1972.

Wright, Dorothy. *Baskets and Basketry.* Great Britain: Redwood, Burn, Limited, 1972.

———— *A Caneworker's Book for the Senior Basketmaker.* Northgates, Leicester, England: Dryad Press, 1970.

Underhill, Ruth. *Pueblo Crafts.* Washington D.C.: U.S. Dept. of the Interior, 1944.

Plants

Blakeslee, Albert F. and Jarvis, Chester D. *Northeastern Trees in Winter:* New York: Dover, 1972.

Britton, Nathaniel Lord Ph.D., Sc.D, L.L.D and Hon. Addison Brown A.B., L.L.D. *Illustrated Flora of Northeastern U.S., Vols. I, II, III.* New York: Dover, 1963.

Densmore, Francis. *How Indians Use Wild Plants for Food, Medicine, and Crafts.* New York: Dover, 1974.

Grimm, William Carey. *The Book of Trees.* Harrisburg, Pennsylvania: Telegraph Press, 1962.

———— *How to Recognize the Shrubs.* New York: Castle Books, 1966.

Harlow, William M. *Trees of the Eastern and Central U.S. and Canada.* New York: Dover, 1957.

Hitchcock, A.S. *Manual of the Grasses of the U.S., Vols. I, II.* New York: Dover, 1971.

Hotchkiss, Neil. *Common Marsh, Underwater, and Floating Leaved Plants.* New York: Dover, 1970.

Keeler, Harriet. *Our Northern Shrubs and How to Identify Them.* New York: Dover, 1969.

Mathews, F. Schuyler. *Field Book of American Trees and Shrubs.* New York: G.P. Putnam's Sons, 1915.

Niering, William A. and Goodwin, Richard H. *Inland Wetland Plants of Connecticut.* Connecticut Arboretum, Bulletin No. 19, Connecticut College, New London, Conn., 1973.

Peattie, Donald C. *A Natural History of Trees of Eastern and Central North America*. New York: Houghton Mifflin Co., 1966.

Dyeing

Adrosko, Rita J. *Natural Dyes and Home Dying*. New York: Dover, 1971.

Davidson, Mary Frances. *The Dye Pot*. Gatlinburg, Tennessee: M.F. Davidson, 1950.

Feder, Norman. *Indian Vegetable Dyes*. Part I and Part II, Leaflet 63 and Leaflet 71. Denver, Colorado: Denver Art Museum, Dept. of Indian Art, reprinted 1969.

Kierstad, Sallie Pease. *Natural Dyes*. Boston: Bruce Humphries, Inc., 1950.

Krochmal, Arnold and Connie. *The Complete Illustrated Book of Dyes from Natural Sources*. New York: Doubleday, 1974.
Meyer, Joseph E. *The Herbalist*. Clarence Mayer, 1973.

Schetky, Ethel Jane MCD (Ed.). *Dye Plants and Dying — A Handbook*. Plants and Gardens, Vol. 20 No. 3. Brooklyn, New York: Brooklyn Botanic Gardens, 1964.

Weigle, Palmy. *Ancient Dyes for Modern Weavers*. New York: Watson-Guptill, 1974.

——— (Ed.). *Natural Plant Dying, A Handbook*. Plants and Gardens Vol. 29, No. 2. Brooklyn, New York: Brooklyn Botanic Gardens, 1974.

Index

Carol Hart grew up in Marin County, California, where the fields, beaches, and mountains inspired her interest in natural science. Her interest in art began as soon as she could hold a crayon and has always been a major part of her life.

She began making baskets and teaching as part of an Indian Studies Program at the Pratt Education Center in 1970. Her initial interest in Eastern Indian Woodland styles led to experimenting with natural materials and dyes and exploring their possibilities for basket forms and designs.

Carol has taught basketry at the Brookfield Craft Center, the Wesleyan Potters, the Washington Art Association, the Niddy Noddy, and for Craftsmen's Guilds in Connecticut, New Hampshire, Rhode Island, New Jersey, and New York.

Dan Hart was born on a farm in the rolling hills of northwestern Connecticut. His interest in the out-of-doors has led him to a career in the field of environmental education. Dan worked with the National Audubon Society as a teacher-naturalist prior to spending seven years as head of the Eliot Pratt Education Center in New Milford, where he co-authored an outdoor activity manual for teachers entitled *Beyond Your Classroom.* Presently he is director of Drumlin Farm, a major educational facility of the Massachusetts Audubon Society in Lincoln.

Dan is a self-taught photographer, and this book represents his first studio effort. Much of his photographic work is derived from his experiences in the natural world.

Edited by Jennifer Place
Designed by Bob Fillie
Set in 10 point Times Roman by Gerard Associates
Printed and bound by Interstate Book Manufacturers Inc.